DATE			

How to Conquer
the Fear of

PUBLIC SPEAKING
&
OTHER CORONARY THREATS

How to Conquer
the Fear of

PUBLIC SPEAKING
&
OTHER CORONARY THREATS

by
Max D. Isaacson

 FARNSWORTH PUBLISHING COMPANY, INC.
a Longman Group company
Rockville Centre, New York 11570

© 1984 Max D. Isaacson.
All rights reserved.
Published by Farnsworth Publishing Co., Inc.
a Longman Group company.
Rockville Centre, New York 11570.
Library of Congress Catalog Card No. 84-13663.
ISBN 0-87863-221-2.
Manufactured in the United States of America.

Library of Congress Cataloging in Publication Data

Isaacson, Max D.

   Public speaking & other coronary threats.

   1. Public speaking.   I. Title.   II. Title: Public
speaking and other coronary threats.
PN4121.I8   1984   808.5'1   84-13663
ISBN 0-87863-221-2

DEDICATED TO . . .

God and my family!

Elizabeth
Scott
Susan
Steven
Stuart
Paul

ACKNOWLEDGEMENTS

I'm grateful to many persons for their influence on my life and their influence on this book. First, I extend thanks to all of the members of the Esquires Toastmasters Club in Des Moines, Iowa, for their encouragement, constructive criticism and applause during the many years I struggled through a dynamic speech program. Extra special thanks go to Toastmasters Rod Johnston, Jim Hamilton, Bob Jenkins, Dick Clothier, Dorothy Begel, Bob Hand, Bob Mitchell, Bill Cook, Jeff Cassat, Ken Pitcher, Lyman McKee, Goff Joyner, Jim Paye, Jack Springer, Gene Lukavsky, Ken Rasmussen, Charles Johnson, Boyd Nordmark, Gene Severs, Sam Zickefoose, Irving Deihl, Leo Cleeton, Gerald Winget, Leander Harrall, Don Morrison, Neil Longseth, Roger Farrow, Bob Glenn, Larry Huegli and Charles Knodle.

Second, I doff my hat to four Christian ministers who gave me such great support during my formative speaking years — the Reverends Otto Steele, Burton Collier, Leonard Root and Dale Ellsworth.

Third, I owe a deep debt of gratitude to the members of the National Speakers Association for their guidance and help with this book.

Additional thanks go to the individuals and publishers listed below:

Material from *Brigance's Speech Communication* by J. Jeffery Auer, reprinted by permission of Prentice-Hall, Inc. Copyright, 1967, by Meredith Publishing Company.

Poem from *The Kleinknecht Gems of Thought Encyclopedia* by Robert Beck, reprinted by permission of C. Fred Kleinknecht. Copyright, 1969, by C. F. Kleinknecht.

Material from *Personhood* by Leo F. Buscaglia, reprinted by permission of SLACK INCORPORATED. Copyright, 1978, by Charles B. Slack, Inc.

Material from *How to Get People to Do Things* by Robert Conklin, reprinted by permission of Contemporary Books, Inc. Copyright, 1979, by Robert Conklin.

Material from *AN ANATOMY OF AN ILLNESS As Perceived by the Patient* by Norman Cousins, reprinted by permission of W. W. Norton & Company, Inc. Copyright, 1979, by W. W. Norton & Company, Inc.

Material from *Enjoyment of Laughter* by Max Eastman, reprinted by permission of Simon & Schuster, Inc. Copyright, 1936, 1963, by Max Eastman.

Material from *"A Motivated Staff Is Your Best Asset"* by N. Donald Edwards, reprinted by permission of *The Typographer.* Copyright, 1983, by Typographers International Association.

Material from *"The Peak Performers"* by Charles A. Garfield, reprinted from *INSIGHT* by permission of Nightingale-Conant Corporation. Copyright, 1983, by Nightingale-Conant Corporation.

Material from *"Stagefright"* by Naomi Graffman, reprinted by permission of Naomi Graffman and *Horizon Magazine*, Volume 24, No. 9, September, 1981. Copyright, 1981, by Horizon Publishers, Inc.

Material from *Public Speaking Without Fear & Trembling* by Mark Hanna, reprinted by permission of Macmillan Publishing Company, Inc. Copyright, 1949, by Macmillan Publishing Company, Inc.

TABLE OF CONTENTS

Acknowledgements

Foreword...MARCH!

Chapter 1
THE OPPORTUNITY IS YOURS!
"Public speaking can be fun!"

Chapter 2
WHY YOU SHOULD WANT TO BE
A GOOD PUBLIC SPEAKER
"Heaven is offering you a rose; and you cling to a cabbage."

Chapter 3
CONFIDENCE CAN BE ACQUIRED
"I want to but I'm scared right out of my pants!"

Chapter 4
HERE'S ADDITIONAL REINFORCEMENT
*"Maybe you think of yourself as a caterpillar
when you've really become a butterfly."*

Chapter 5
HOW FAMOUS PERSONS COPE
"It's spit-up time."

Chapter 6
A PROGRAM FOR REALIZING YOUR GOALS
"After you get where you're going, where will you be?"

Chapter 7
HOW AND WHERE TO IMPROVE
YOUR PUBLIC SPEAKING
"Life is now in session — are you present?"

Chapter 8
HOW TO PREPARE A SPEECH
"I don't dance, but I'd love to hold you while you do."
ANALYZE YOUR AUDIENCE
USE APPROPRIATE MATERIAL
GESTURES & VOCAL VARIETY
SHOULD I USE NOTES?
WHAT ABOUT VISUAL AIDS?
ATTENTION-GETTING OPENINGS
MEMORABLE CLOSINGS

Chapter 9
WHAT ABOUT HUMOR?
"He who laughs, lasts."

Chapter 10
SO YOU'VE ACCEPTED AN INVITATION TO SPEAK?
The Audience Asks: "What's in it for me?"
CHECKING THE FACILITIES
INTRODUCING YOU
DON'T FORGET TO LISTEN
DON'T UNDERESTIMATE YOUR AUDIENCE
INVOLVING THE AUDIENCE
HOW IMPORTANT IS THE WAY I DRESS?
GETTING AN HONEST CRITIQUE

Chapter 11
SPEAK PROFESSIONALLY — AND GET PAID!
"Money is not the root of all evil."
HOW MUCH SHOULD I CHARGE?
TIPS ON A PERSONAL BROCHURE
ANALYZING THE MARKET

Chapter 12
PERSONAL FULFILLMENT THROUGH SPEAKING
"May you live all the days of your life."

Foreword...MARCH!

"I'm surprised that the phobia surrounding Public Speaking is at the top of the list of those things we all agonize over ... I'm convinced that fear is not so much a phobia as it is an excuse we often use for our own unwillingness to *try*."

Rod McKuen

Chapter 1

The Opportunity Is Yours!

International Order Of Positive Speakers
3RD ANNUAL CONVENTION

"Public speaking can be fun!"

I saw a billboard message the other day that zapped me. It said: ***"There's no heavier burden than a great opportunity."*** How incisive! And that's exactly how I feel about public speaking and all that it has to offer. It's a heavy burden for those who want to capitalize on it.

If you're like most people who want to be good public speakers, you have a fear of it. I did and still do! It may surprise you to know that a very large percentage of professional speakers and entertainers also have an on-going fear of public speaking. But the object of this book is to share with you **how** they and others who are non-professional have learned to *control* this fear and how they have learned to make it work in a positive way for their benefit and the benefit of their audiences.

Note that I don't say they have **overcome** their fear of public speaking. Most people, I've learned, don't overcome it. They do, however, learn to **manage** it in such a way that it ultimately becomes nothing more than a desirable stimulant to their presentations. In other words, **they have conquered the fear of fear!**

Let's be honest with ourselves. Won't you admit that it's silly to **fear** public speaking? Why fear something that can be controlled with a little effort? Whatever your age **(I was 37 when I decided to do something about it)** I know beyond the shadow of a doubt that you can learn not only to manage your fear of public speaking but you can grow into a fully-confident person who will find that an enhanced public-speaking ability is an extremely important step to future accomplishments.

EXCUSE AFTER EXCUSE

Please don't think this is some kind of snow job because it isn't! I used to be so scared in front of a group that I would go to any extreme to avoid it. Yes, I used to make excuse after excuse — which obviously made me feel absolutely rotten and terribly inferior.

However, I got sick and tired of that miserable feeling of being unable to address an audience without shaking in my shoes. I was like the guy who was so self-conscious that he couldn't even lead a group in *silent* prayer. I guess it took a little faith in my Creator as well as in my peers to convince me that Ralph Waldo Emerson was right when he said, "Do the thing you fear and the death of it is certain."

Many others who have achieved worthwhile goals have reflected the same philosophy, including the renowned scientist Marie Curie, who observed, "Nothing in life is to be feared. It is only to be understood."

You will gain self-confidence as you gain more knowledge of

this subject and as you come to accept the fact that there is no insurmountable barrier in public speaking.

I hope you believe that! I do! And if you believe that I had something special in my genes that you don't, that I didn't have the usual adult apprehensions about earning a decent living, that I was forced into speech training by an employer, that I had some mystical experience to prod me — think again.

ON OVERCOMING ADVERSITY

My father was a coal miner with a fourth-grade education. My mother had not gone beyond seventh grade. Although they were beautiful human beings and wonderful parents, they did not express much self-confidence nor did they instill an appreciation of self-confidence in me (I was the youngest of six children). I grew up during the Great Depression of the 1930s without any financial security. I lacked self-esteem.

Let me give you several reasons why I lacked self-esteem: I suffered from enuresis until the age of 12; because we were relatively poor, I lived with crooked front teeth until I reached adulthood; my parents never had enough money to purchase their own auto, so we never took vacations as my peers did; within our family, hand-me-down clothing was the rule.

Prior to my first year in high school, my parents looked at two school possibilities. One high school was across town in a lower- to middle-class neighborhood; the other, which I also *could* have attended, was closer to my home and in a well-to-do neighborhood. Guess which one they sent me to? They thought the former was better suited to "our middle-class status" and they didn't think it would be wise for me to mix "with the rich kids." Needless to say, their reasoning didn't help my ego but what really hurt was their inability to see the possibilities in aiming higher in life, or to communicate that to me.

Then, in later adult life, I worked for a number of employers who didn't have the slightest interest in any staff member developing his or her self-esteem or in improving his or her public speaking ability. Although I'm a regular church-goer, I have not had any special spiritual motivation to overcome this hangup, this phobia of public speaking. Moreover, I've had ulcers, so I wasn't looking for additional stressful situations.

MOTIVATING FORCE

Well, then, you might wonder, what did prompt me to carry out a planned program of self-improvement through public speaking? I believe the strongest motivating force was the knowledge that **the ability to express oneself well CAN make a difference in your earnings, your self-respect, your happiness and your world.** I had no one to blame for my apprehension and no one to blame for not doing something about it. Do you blame your parents, your employer or our society for the shortcomings you might have?

To help me in my struggle with self-doubt as it applied to public speaking, I read most of the books on the subject of positive thinking. I read a great deal of scripture, looking for encouragement. I analyzed the speeches and delivery of well-known persons. I accumulated a lot of knowledge on the subject but the one thing I failed to do was *to put it into practice!* Believe me, the first step was a difficult one. So was the second, and the third. But the more steps you take, the easier it becomes.

Michael Korda, a successful businessman, tells about the fear of failing in a recent article in *Success* magazine: "Many of us feel, profoundly and unconsciously, that 'the higher you climb, the harder you fall,' and solve the problem by not climbing at all."

I'm sure we've all known moments in our lives when we hesitated to climb because we feared the consequences. But I believe that sometimes we need to crawl out on a limb to feel the thrill of risk-taking. These risks may be big or they may be small. And sometimes we indeed are "hurt" by a fall but I like what Florence Nightingale said: "Better to have pain than paralysis."

In my own adult life I have many times agonized over certain courses of action because I felt I would be risking my pride, if not my finances. And every time I face a difficult decision in my life (and deciding to tackle public speaking certainly was one) I try to remember that the philosopher Johann Wolfgang von Goethe observed, "Everybody wants to be somebody; nobody wants to grow."

A CHALLENGE FOR OUR TIME

So this book is about growing — to a certain extent — because I feel it's a challenge for our time. A national study conducted a few years ago stated that what most people want — young or old — is not merely security, or comfort, or luxury. Most of all, they want *meaning* in their lives . . . objectives, convictions, substance, direction! So I would ask the question that I ask in some of my public presentations: "After you get where you're going, where will YOU be?"

Victor Hugo told us that "People do not lack strength; they lack will." Sometimes we're like the teenage boy who was madly in love with a girl and as they were walking home from their first date, the boy wanted desperately to give her a kiss, but being a religious youngster, he said out loud: "Father, father up above, should I kiss the girl I love?" And a big, booming voice came from out of the sky and said: "Sinner, sinner down below; pucker up and let her go!"

If you want to be a public speaker, I hope you, too, will "pucker up and let her go!" You're risking much less than you might think — and the reachable goals are much more rewarding than you think.

In addition to my own public speaking, I occasionally schedule other professional speakers for various kinds of conferences and annual meetings. I recently scheduled a speaker with a most unusual background.

THE "GREAT IMPOSTER"

His name is Frank Abagnale. Frank is known as the "great imposter; the world's greatest con artist; the man who successfully posed as a pilot, a pediatrician, an assistant attorney general, a stockbroker, a college professor, and an FBI agent." He cashed 2½ million dollars in phony checks, in all 50 states and 26 foreign countries. He subsequently paid the price for his wrongdoings by being imprisoned for several years, both in

France and in the United States.

Today, his life's goal is to help eliminate white collar crime in order to help repay his debt to society. He has appeared on national television numerous times to tell his life's story. His book *(Catch Me If You Can)* has sold about two million copies and plans are being made for a movie version of his life.

He makes 200 speeches a year world-wide. Before his speech to a banking group in my home town, I chatted with him about fear in his life and how one might go about gaining more self-confidence, particularly in the field of public speaking.

Frank told me that if we really try, we can take a liability and turn it into an asset. "In my own life," he said, "I had this terrible record of crime to live down but whenever I tried to get a job after my release from prison, employers remembered who I was and rejected me. Finally, my parole officer suggested that I take this negative thing and turn it into something positive. That's how I got started making public presentations."

Frank, too, echoes Emerson's advice: "I really believe you have to **do** the thing you fear to overcome it, and frequently it's a very difficult step to take. No one can do it for you."

PROCEED CONFIDENTLY

Look again at his last statement: *No one can do it for you!* Proceed now, confidently. You aren't expected to go to the moon, or to win an Oscar, or to revolutionize the art of public speaking. Just stick your neck out a little — risk it!

"Until one is committed," said Goethe, "there is hesitancy, the chance to draw back to ineffectiveness. The moment one definitely commits oneself," he said, *"then Providence moves, too.* Whatever you can do or dream you can, begin it. *Boldness has genius power and magic in it."*

This book has been written from the viewpoint of a person who actually passed through a critical period in his life. There is nothing in this book that is difficult to comprehend or to apply in your own life. It is not a heavy academic or psychological treatment of the subject. It's a *practical* book. This is a book that can help you. This is a book that was born of my own frustration and subsequent accomplishment. It's an honest book — and I firmly believe everything that it contains. Moreover, I believe that even the most shy person can speak with relative confidence to a group of people if that person is willing to exercise enough self-discipline to follow my suggestions.

Accept the fact, won't you, that *you can learn to be an effective public speaker! It doesn't take much to start on that road to your goal! It just takes desire!* Leave the rest to me and to your own intuition. And be honest with yourself, too, in the process.

Admit that you want to be more confident. Admit that you want to be able to influence those around you through your speaking ability. Admit that most days **you communicate ORALLY more than in any other way!** *TAKE THIS BOOK IN YOUR HAND. HOLD IT TO YOUR HEART AND BELIEVE IN YOUR HEAD THAT THE TIME IS NOW! DON'T BE AFRAID. DO IT!*

What are you going to get out of it if you do take it to heart? I'll tell you — you're going to find that you are going to feel a heck of a lot better about yourself. You're going to find yourself not only speaking up but WANTING to in the various groups to which you belong, whether they be scouting organizations, church groups, business conferences or political clubs. YOU'RE GOING TO MAKE YOU PROUD OF YOU!

> **The heights by great men reached and kept**
> **Were not attained by sudden flight,**
> **But they, while their companions slept,**
> **Were toiling upward in the night.**
> *Longfellow*

"Our doubts are traitors, and make us lose the good we oft might win by fearing to attempt."
WILLIAM SHAKESPEARE

"If, when you look into your own heart, you find nothing wrong there, what is there to worry about, what is there to fear?"
CONFUCIUS

"Did you ever hear of a man who had striven all his life faithfully and singly toward an object and in no measure obtained it? If a man constantly aspires, is he not elevated?"
HENRY DAVID THOREAU

"Find an aim in life before you run out of ammunition."
ARNOLD GLASOW

"My epitaph will be just two words: 'I tried.' "
MICKEY ROONEY

"The great dividing line between success and failure can be expressed in five words, 'I did not have time.'"
ROBERT J. HASTINGS

"We spend 80% of our waking day communicating, and few of us do it well. But it's the key to life."
LILLIAN GLASS, Communications Specialist
Quoted in *USA Today*

"The virtue of all achievement is victory over oneself. Those who know this victory can never know defeat."
A.J. CRONIN

"I thank God for my handicaps, for, through them, I have found myself, my work, and my God."
HELEN KELLER

Chapter 2

Why You Should Want To Be A Good Public Speaker

"Heaven is offering you a rose; and you cling to a cabbage."

"By the magic of the spoken word, we tip men's minds out of bed, stab their spirits awake, and set them on the forward march for a better personal, professional and business life. All who hear us can be a little wiser, walk a little taller, live and serve a little better. We have a matchless opportunity to affect the quality of life at this challenging point in time."

That statement by Carl Winters, a past president of the National Speakers Association, is one of those that I wish I had made. Yes, the spoken word can build bridges or barriers to our fellow man.

Since we communicate orally so much of each day (one source says the average person speaks about 30,000 words daily), I've always thought that there should be greater emphasis on this subject in our public educational systems and throughout commerce and government. In high school, college, military service, graduate school and after 25 years in business, I found that any emphasis on better oral communications has been conspicuous by its absence.

SOMETHING TO SAY

While no one would deny the importance of effective one-to-one communication, we will be stressing in this book the need for effective oral communications on a **public** basis. When I say "public" I mean to any group — large or small — outside of one's own family. Such a group might be in a formal setting or an informal one. The speaker is there because he or she has something to say and — presumably — the group wants to hear it.

I believe the majority of public speakers today use a conversational style whereas the oratory of yesteryear was presented with great affectation (some preachers and politicians today might be the exceptions to the rule).

Most persons can see the need for lawyers, teachers and clergymen to study public speaking but many wonder whether it's all that important to businessmen, doctors, students, farmers and housewives. Consider, though, how important effective speech can be in sales work, company training programs, public relations, political rallies, church functions, fund-raising programs, city hall meetings, after-dinner presentations, and so on.

Moreover, there is a plethora of civic and trade associations requiring leadership, and leadership means presiding at meetings and *speaking* in public. A nationally-known management consultant made a rather dramatic statement recently when he said, **"Your image and advancement depend more on your communication skills than on your actual ability."** THINK

ABOUT THAT FOR A MOMENT AND READ HIS STATEMENT AGAIN. Many believe your speech is the most vital part of your equipment for success, for winning what you want in life.

STANFORD RESEARCH

If you doubt that, consider this, which was reported in the November/December 1983 issue of *Personal Selling Power:* "Stanford Research Institute says that the money you make in any line of endeavor is determined only 12½% by knowledge and 87½% by your ability to deal with people. The Carnegie Foundation spent one million dollars over a five year period for research that proved that only 15% of a person's ability to get a job, keep a job and move ahead in that job was due to knowledge and 85% was due to his or her ability to deal with people."

Indeed, our nation's executives now believe in giving speech training priority in light of their own hangups, because they want future leaders to reflect self-confidence and to present a better company image. Not long ago, the *Wall Street Journal* reported, "One of top executives' greatest fears is public speaking. Presidents, chief executive officers and board chairmen may find it easy to direct huge corporations. But put them before an audience, and their authority diminishes. They are alone, being judged as individuals, and they are uncomfortable."

HISTORICALLY SPEAKING

Just how important is speech? "Speech is civilization itself," said Thomas Mann. "The word, even the most contradictory word, preserves contact."

The study of public speaking supposedly began about 500 B.C. when two men, Corax and Tisias, went into the law courts in the city of Syracus on the island of Sicily. They observed the manner of speech-making and made notes of the speeches which were effective and those which were ineffective. They analyzed both kinds of speeches to determine their reasons for success or failure.

In his book *Brigance's SPEECH COMMUNICATION,* J. Jeffery Auer tells us, "Throughout all of history speech has been viewed as a social force by means of which man interprets, controls, modifies, or adapts to his environment. 'None of the things which are done with intelligence,' wrote Isocrates, about 400 B.C., 'are done without the aid of speech.' In our own day Bishop Gerald Kennedy, of the Los Angeles Area of the United Methodist Church, declares that 'the spoken word is still the most powerful instrument for shaping society and affecting lives.' And on the international scene André Maurois, Nobel prize winner and member of the French Academy, dramatizes the notion by affirming that as 'contemporary leaders still have the power to voice the fears and hopes and stir the hearts of men; one speech may be worth three divisions.' "

Are you beginning to see the need for better oral communications in your life? If you still have doubts, consider the following:

Daniel Webster said, "If all my possessions were taken from me with one exception, I would choose to keep the power of speech, for by it I would soon regain all the rest (of my possessions)."

Sigmund Freud observed, "Words call forth emotions and are universally the means by which we influence our fellow creatures . . . by words, one of us can give to another the greatest happiness or bring about utter despair."

The eminent **Dale Carnegie** asserted, "Every activity of our lives is communication of a sort, but it is through speech that man asserts his distinctiveness . . . that he best expresses his own individuality, his essence."

Winston Churchill said, "Words are the only weapons we've got."

Senator J. W. Fullbright claimed, "Communication is power."

However, it might surprise you to know that one of our generation's greatest communicators — Marshall McLuhan

— says, "Far from being normal, *successful* communication is a rarity."

SPEECH, OUR GREATEST GIFT

Lester Thonssen and Ross Scanlan touch on speech clarity in their book *Speech Preparation and Delivery,* "Most of the mistaken ideas about public speaking grow out of the word 'public,' " they write. "Certainly no one would accept that speaking alone was an activity important only to lawyers, teachers, and clergymen. Stripped of the word 'public,' it becomes apparent that speaking is necessary in practically every occupation. Regardless of the kind of work that is being done, speech is frequently needed to make something clear to others with whom one is working, or to convince them that something is true or false, or to show that something should or should not be done. And, since speaking is necessary to carry on work in most walks of life, the ability to speak well is necessary, for 'to speak well' simply means to succeed in the purpose for speaking."

But again — why speak *in public*? There are a lot of reasons but mainly because **you have something to say**. Perhaps you want to impress your boss, spouse, political caucus, scout troop or those gathered to toast newly-weds. Maybe you are in a specific public relations capacity with your employer — private or public. For example, my friends Bob Glenn and Neil Longseth expended great effort on public speaking when they were troopers representing my state's highway patrol. It helped them tremendously when they had to make public service announcements or had to lead training sessions. Today, in non-government roles, they still are making dynamic presentations to audiences.

If you've ever squirmed at a public meeting because you had an opinion on a subject but were afraid of experiencing that naked feeling, of having attention focused on you, you have one of a thousand reasons for learning how to speak confidently and effectively.

ELIMINATE THE COP-OUTS

If you've ever wanted to lead any organization, to make your position known on a public issue, to conduct a Bible class, to seek a promotion — you owe it to yourself to make the effort to become an acceptable (if not an outstanding) public speaker. Eliminate the cop-outs, like "I'm too shy;" "It's really not my cup of tea;" "I'm not knowledgeable on that subject;" "Let George do it."

I think it's safe to say that speeches are given for three general purposes: To *inform,* to *entertain* or to *persuade.* Some speeches obviously incorporate more than one purpose, such as an informative speech that combines certain entertainment features. You may not feel qualified to tackle all three purposes initially but you certainly do have opinions on issues which can be shared with others.

Most of us have at least average intelligence, and when we look around us — at co-workers, bosses, politicians, opinion formulators — we know that our level of knowledge is as great or greater than theirs, but the thing that so often separates us is our inability to feel confident when expressing ourselves. We fear to speak up.

It's true that we make ourselves vulnerable when we speak up . . . vulnerable to criticism. It's usually easier and more comfortable to stay out of the spotlight and to languish in the safety of the nonspeaker's role. It's less risky, isn't it? But we can't avoid feeling a little inferior because of our hesitancy to speak up.

I've always been fond of quoting Eleanor Roosevelt on the subject of self-confidence and it was she who said, **"No one can make you feel inferior without your consent."** Isn't that a remarkable statement? So stop consenting and start asserting.

SPEAKING IS NOT A SPECTATOR SPORT

Mrs. Roosevelt also left us these words of wisdom, "The purpose of life, after all, is to live it, to taste experience to the utmost, to reach out eagerly and without fear for newer and richer experience."

Or, as Dr. Robert H. Schuller admonishes us, **"It takes guts to leave the ruts."**

William James, who lived from 1842 to 1910 and who has been called the father of American psychology, liked to point out that we find meaning in life not by being bystanders but by becoming participants in the drama of human existence. "Be not afraid of life," he said. "Believe that life is worth living, and your belief will create the fact."

Abraham Lincoln said, "The older I get the more I realize that there is but one wealth, one security, on this earth and that is found in the ability of a person to perform a task well. And first and foremost this ability must start with knowledge."

Yes, you need knowledge of public speaking if you are to do an *exceptional* job of speaking. I don't believe anyone wants to be *mediocre* at anything so it is essential that you obtain all the beneficial information you can on this subject.

You see, it's not enough to just research the subject. You need the right resource material and I believe this book can help you tremendously if you use it in conjunction with serious practice.

My high school basketball coach — Glenn R. (Bodge) Bowles — used to tell us: "Practice doesn't make perfect, but *perfect* practice does." I hope to show you some perfect or near perfect ways to practice your speech making for more satisfying results. In other words, practice the **right** things. One of the keys is getting constructive feedback, but we'll get more into that later in the book.

A LIVING LEGEND

One of this nation's outstanding public speakers and speech mentors is Cavett Robert, one of the founders of the National Speakers Association. Cavett truly is a legend in his own time. He writes, "A constructive life is built of the things we do — not of the things we don't do. I once heard a person who was being criticized make the remark, 'I know my way is not perfect but I like the way I do it better than the way you *don't* do it.' Never forget that the only material which can be used in building a life is positive action. Negative inaction is valueless in constructing anything except criticisms and excuses."

For other inspiring material, I strongly recommend his book *Success With People Through Human Engineering and Motivation.*

Another book which caught my eye recently is Ben Stein's *Bunkhouse Logic.* Stein says, and I certainly concur, **"There is no happiness without self-esteem.** What is it? How do you get it? To be happy, one must be happy with oneself. In real life that comes from accomplishments of which one can be proud."

He continues, "High self-esteem can enable anyone to break out of any rut and move toward triumph. No matter what forces are arrayed against a man or woman with high self-esteem, he or she can defeat them. This is a self-fulfilling prophecy." Stein says that "even a small measure of real-life accomplishment is a far stronger benefit to the soul than any number of hours of whining in a room lined with bookcases, modern art, and diplomas."

YOU EARN IT

If one is to achieve excellence in public speaking, it will take effort. If you haven't read John W. Gardner's book *Excellence* you've missed a great publication. I find that it carries the seeds for better public speaking. Gardner says, "All excellence involves discipline and tenacity of purpose." But don't let that discourage you, because he adds, "For there *is* something to the idea that the surmounting of hardships strengthens character. There *is* something to the notion that 'difficulty is the nurse of greatness.' "

Your attitude, your individual effort is the key. Who could argue with Ralph Waldo Emerson, who told us, "Make the most of yourself, for that is all there is of you."

In his book *Personhood* Dr. Leo F. Buscaglia makes a similar point: "Elie Wiesel tells us of a rabbi who has said that when we cease to live and go before our Creator the question asked of us will not be why we did not become a messiah, a famous leader or to answer the great mysteries of life. The question will be simply — why did you not become you, the fully active, realized person that only you had the potential of becoming.

"Where do we start? We start at the present moment. We abandon the past and embrace the now. We start with the most valued possession and our only possession which can lead us to our own personal full humanity. We take the wise advice of Wiesel's rabbi, 'We start with ourselves.'

"We are faced with the reality that if we wish to live fully and in harmony with life, we will have to become self-motivated students. We will have to be ready to risk, look inside ourselves, and proceed through trial and error. The job will be mainly ours. We will be required to be our own mentors."

THERE ARE GREAT REWARDS

I hope you are ready to risk some of your pride in order to become an effective public speaker. Remember — you cannot **not** communicate. Even your silence is communication. But how much more fulfilling your life can be if you will but shed your inhibitions about public speaking, because there are great rewards for the effort. Don't forget, though, the old folk saying that "God provides the nuts, but you've got to crack them if you want to eat."

Opportunities in public speaking are everywhere and I encourage you to grab them now! A statement in a G.B. Shaw play sums up the way I feel about it, **"Heaven is offering you a rose; and you cling to a cabbage."** Don't cling to your cabbage — reach for a rose.

So often we ask life's challenges: What's in it for me? I believe the rewards will be far greater than you can imagine at the moment. Dale Carnegie taught public speaking for years and his book *How To Develop Self-Confidence and Influence People By Public Speaking* is one I sincerely believe to be the benchmark to which all other publications on this subject should be measured. Carnegie said, "I know hundreds of men who have created more prestige by one five-minute talk than they had by five years of grinding work. Once successfully master an audience with a short talk and thereafter you'll be a better master of yourself."

He added, "I have traveled around the world several times, but I know of few things that give greater delight than holding an audience by the power of the spoken word."

Why speak in public? Perhaps poet Dorothy R. Jones expressed it best when she wrote:

> **"Your task — to build a better**
> **world,"**
>   **God said.**
> **I answered, "How?**
> **The world is such a large, vast**
> **place,**
>   **So complicated now.**
> **And I so small and useless am,**
>   **There's nothing I can do**
> **But God in all His wisdom said,**
>   **"Just build a better you."**

"It is a great misfortune not to have sense enough to speak well."

ERASMUS

"There is no index of character so sure as the voice."

DISRAELI

"Your body is the harp of the soul. And it is yours to bring forth from it sweet music or confused sounds..."

KAHLIL GIBRAN

"Except ye utter by the tongue words easy to be understood, how shall it be known what is spoken?"

I CORINTHIANS, 14:9

"Every man should be able to do something all by himself — something that gives him a sense of mastery: Fly, sing, write, bake a good loaf of bread, handle a Bowie knife, tap dance, find new star, carve in ivory. Man needs to solo."

BRUCE GOULD

Chapter 3

Confidence Can Be Acquired

"I want to but I'm scared right out of my pants!"

It's incredible but true: Surveys repeatedly have shown that speaking in public is feared more than death, illness or poverty.

Believe me, like most beginning speakers, I, too, used to get really scared! How scared was I? This may sound like a quip from a Johnny Carson monologue, but I've been asked many times: Are you really scared before a speech? In a word, YES! But I can assure you that **the anticipation more often than not is more agonizing than the actual experience.**

But back to the question: How scared was I?

- As a youngster in public school, whenever my English teacher conducted stand-up spelling bees, I used to intentionally misspell words so that I could immediately sit down and not have to continue standing before the class.

- As a young lad in Sunday school, I vividly remember being virtually forced to sing a hymn solo and I became so nervous that I inadvertently sang the same stanza twice, much to the amusement of my peers.

- In college, I always avoided talking before groups if I could. The year that I was editor of my university's student newspaper, I barely was able to hold staff conferences without shaking in my boots.

- As an officer in the military service, I always tried to get a non-com or another officer to conduct military briefings in my place.

- As a young businessman, I at times would feign illness to my boss to escape a public presentation.

- And once I even fibbed to my pastor and told him I had to be out of town on a Sunday when he wanted me to read scripture from the pulpit.

- I've even had near-accidents of a biological nature because of stage fright.

Have you experienced miserable conditions like that? If you have, there's hope. If you haven't, you're a rare bird indeed. Most of us have lots of company, as the saying goes, with our fear of public speaking and in a later chapter I'll share with you information I've received from many personalities who are famous in entertainment, sports, business and broadcasting. They, too, have had and continue to suffer stage fright. But the point is — they manage to control it and achieve their objectives in communicating with audiences effectively.

UNDERSTANDING FEAR

By the way, the word "fear" is of Anglo-Saxon origin and is defined as a painful emotion marked by alarm or the anticipation of danger. Some observers would say the malady more appropriately should be referred to as *shyness* instead of *fearfulness*. However, Webster's dictionary's first definition of *shy*

says that it is a condition of being "easily frightened." Therefore, in this book we'll use the two terms interchangeably but
with greater emphasis on *fearfulness* rather than on *shyness*.

I want to convince you, however, with every ounce of sincerity that I can muster that there really is no danger and you
CAN control the fear (or your shyness) of public speaking.
Granted, you cannot merely wish that this fear or shyness will
vanish — you have to work at it. But the job is not that
difficult. I know of case after case after case to prove it and I
know you can master it if you WANT to badly enough.

There are many dramatic examples of speakers who have
hurdled this barrier and have made names for themselves in
their clubs, their houses of worship, their companies, their
communities and their governmental bodies. But more important, they have overcome a handicap. They have won a major
victory for themselves. They have proved that **the master of
fear or shyness is self-confidence.** Over the years, I've known a
lot of persons who were invited to speak to a public gathering
but they often responded, "I want to but I'm scared right out of
my pants!"

Dr. Louis H. Valbracht, a Lutheran pastor whom I had the
privilege of hearing several years ago, shared the following
story on fear with his congregation: A father, who was being
insistently questioned by his little son, assured the lad that he
was not afraid of the dark, he was not afraid of ghosts nor
goblins, nor monsters, nor thunder, nor lightning, nor atomic
bombs, nor snakes, nor policemen. And the son finally said,
"Gee, Dad, I guess you're not afraid of anything, except
Mother."

ARE YOU AFRAID?

All of us seem to have something that mars our record of
courage, said Dr. Valbracht, adding, "Look around you. Do
you see anyone who is completely unafraid? What about you?
Are you afraid? Of course you are. And so is everyone else. The
fact of fear seems to be one of the facts of life — for everyone —
for fear is no respecter of persons, or positions, or places. No
one is immune to it. A famous physician says: 'The commonest

and most subtle of all human diseases is fear.' Fear of the future, fear of danger, fear of Communism, fear of atom bombs, fear of loss — loss of health, loss of possessions, loss of position, loss of job, loss of self-esteem — fear of failure, fear of ridicule, fear of exposure, fear of being disliked, fear of death, fear of the unknown. 'Where a man can find no answer,' says Norman Cousins, 'he will find fear.' "

Dr. Valbracht then reminded us that Overstreet, the famous psychiatrist, speaks of the peculiar grip of fear. He says, "Of all the emotional forces that pattern our individual and interpersonal behavior, fear has the most insidious power to make us do what we ought to do. Under its influence and trying to escape its influence, we seem fated to give it yet a stronger and stronger hold on us."

What should we do in the face of fear — particularly any fears we might have with regard to public speaking? Dr. Valbracht had some excellent advice, and he certainly was a good one to give it because he was the recipient of many military decorations for his service as a combat chaplain in the Pacific Theater of action during World War II.

He said, "First, face your fears. Look at them. Examine them. See them for what they really are. It's very often the case that they are nonsense, that they are the products of our overactive imaginations and that you are working yourself into a state of agitation over something that will never happen. Then, replace fear with faith. It is never enough just to say: 'Fear, be gone!' Fear must be replaced.

FAITH ANSWERS

"At the time of the Dunkirk disaster back in 1940, you remember how the Nazi armies had moved to the Straits of Dover and how thousands of Englishmen were thrown into a panic waiting for what they thought would be the inevitable invasion of the German armies on their tiny island. At that time, someone wrote over the entrance of a hotel near Dover: 'Fear knocked. Faith answered: "No one is here." ' "

TREAT YOURSELF LIKE A BELOVED FRIEND

In his book *Feeling Good,* David D. Burns tells how one can develop a sense of self-esteem. One of the points he makes is this:

"Decide to treat yourself like a beloved friend. Imagine that some VIP came unexpectedly to visit you. How would you treat the person? You would wear your best clothes, offer your finest food, and do everything you could to make him feel comfortable and pleased. You would be sure to let him know how highly you value him and how honored you are that he chose to spend some time with you. Now — why not treat yourself like that? Do it all the time if you can! After all, in the final analysis, no matter how impressed you are with your favorite VIP, you are more important to you than he is."

A similar philosophy is expressed by Ralph Ransom in his book *Steps on the Stairway.* He poses the question: What will make us move toward something we want? What will spur us into action to get what we desire? He says thousands of people enter goals programs each year and are told to list all the things they want, then to write out a plan of action and to begin working on it. But, says Ransom, nothing really happens, even though they make elaborate plans of action.

Why don't they reach the goal? Why the reluctance to take the necessary steps for success? Here's what the author has to say:

"People may be theoretically capable, but most are not even remotely willing to pay the price. It becomes clearer and clearer that many men and women are nowhere close to being self-motivators. Their goals are very weak and this is the way they want it . . . . The great tragedy is that man was created as a being who should constantly keep improving, a being who on reaching one goal sets a higher one. He must always be activating his potential. He is in a state of becoming."

He adds that most people studying success books, motivation courses and inspirational literature are hoping to acquire a better job, a new home or a more expensive car.

WE BECOME THE TREASURE

"But we are the final product of the eight steps," asserts Ransom. "All things are secondary to that. We become the treasure. If not, all has been a waste of time. Nothing outside you can be as valuable as you. You didn't just stumble onto the great treasures of life, or find them by accident. You found them because you were searching for them. The easy shortcuts to success lead nowhere."

You may think that your particular personality is so different that there's no way that you could speak confidently to a large audience. Please don't be misled in your thinking. Dr. Harry Emerson Fosdick removes any crutch we might be leaning on with this observation: **"Three elements enter into the building of a personality: heredity, environment and personal response. We are not responsible for our heredity; much of our environment we cannot control; but the power to face life with our individual rejoinder — *that* we are responsible for."**

Let me tell you a remarkable story about a remarkable man — Don Ross. Don is the president of a huge national information-processing firm that specializes in service to major magazine publishers and users of direct mail.

Several years ago, Don was scheduled to present a paper at an important client seminar in Chicago. As he began his presentation, he started to shake uncontrollably. He excused himself from the conference and flew back to company headquarters. He felt terribly frustrated and embarrassed. You don't get to feeling much lower than Don did that day.

Eventually, however, Don came to realize that there was no stigma in getting knocked down, figuratively speaking. The stigma was only in lying there and not doing anything about it. And he did do something about it. He joined a Toastmasters club and subsequently became a very effective public speaker. The last time we met publicly, he was scheduled to introduce me as the banquet's main speaker. He did a superb job and is a living testimonial to the "I can" community of positive thinkers.

JIM MESTON'S ACHIEVEMENTS

Another living testimonial is Jim Meston of Pittsburgh, Pa. Jim was a very good athlete at the university I attended but I had lost track of him these past 30 years. Then just the other day, I chanced to read Maury White's sports column in our local Des Moines *Register*. Here's what he had to say about Jim Meston:

"Drake [University] has a classy Double D Award for former lettermen who, in effect, have also won letters in later life. Last Thursday's recipients were Dale Bennett of Maitland, Fla.; Carl Johannsen of Burlington, Ia.; McCoy McLemore of Houston, Texas, and Jim Meston of Pittsburgh, Pa.

"Earning success and respect in chosen occupation, rather than simply having made a great deal of money, is the major criterion. Of the four, I plan to zero in on Meston because, if you'll excuse the expression, he has succeeded despite a stuttering start.

"Starting at age 6 for reasons that have yet to be made clear to him, the Des Moines native developed an outstanding case of tangle tongue. Saying his own name was sheer torture. 'Hello' became a 30-second journey. The thought of ever arising to speak in public was as remote as whatever galaxy is 100 billion light years removed from our own.

" 'What happened to me just didn't seem fair,' says a Dowling High School graduate, whose father and grandfather both toiled for *The Register*. 'When you're a Catholic kid and go to confession, you change your voice. Except you can't, if you stutter. People often ask, "Have you stuttered all your life?" I say, "not yet." '

IT'S CONQUERABLE

"Life being what it is, meaning conquerable, you will be happy to know that the still-tangle tongued

Meston is Director, Human Resources for Westinghouse. He makes many speeches each year for his primary employer, does maybe a dozen more at a very high level on vacation time and, for the last 12 years, has furnished the humor at Pittsburgh's annual Dapper Dan banquet, one of the nation's largest sports celebrity events.

"And to show how a person can benefit from good friends made along the way, one of the first non-Westinghouse tycoons to hire Meston to orally motivate a business group was former Bulldog teammate Tom Bienemann, the president of Speedo International, a Portland-based sportswear firm best known for outfitting competitive swim stars.

" 'Years ago, I set the standard for Jim's national fee, which is a good one,' said Bienemann, previously a top executive with several other clothing manufacturers. 'And the first time I showed up with a stutterer, a lot of my associates thought I'd flipped. Two minutes after starting, Jim had the group in the palm of his hand.'

"Thirty years ago, Bienemann would have been certifiably nuts, but Jim has come a long way. As many stutterers, Meston senses not being able to say a certain word and deftly substitutes another. These days, he often gets out a lot of words without even a noticeable pause. But sometimes he doesn't. Instead of panic, he somehow turns this into charm.

" 'I can speak to 5,000 people now and not be a bit nervous,' he points out. 'But if I know I'm going to have to say my name out loud, my palms start sweating. When you say your name, you don't have the option of switching words.'

"Serendipity is the finding of agreeable things not sought. Bienemann, an earlier recipient of the Double D, came to see Meston receive the award. Tom had called and suggested we have breakfast, then kindly brought Meston along.

WON SEVEN LETTERS

"Original intentions were to write about Biene-mann, one of my favorite humans. Tom won seven letters as a Bulldog, four in football, the last in 1950 when John Bright was a junior, and set many pass catching records. As a pro, he was six seasons with the Cardinals as a defensive end and linebacker.

"Just as did Bright, Bienemann came to Drake on a basketball scholarship. Tom lettered twice in basketball, also once in baseball as a catcher and he and Meston got to laughing about the baseball letter that each *didn't* get.

" 'When we were seniors in 1951, Shan Deniston, the baseball coach, told us not to play in the Alumni football game. We didn't intend to, because we'd played a doubleheader in the afternoon, but some of the guys got on us and we suited up that night and played Bright and the underclassmen. Beat the hell out of them, too,' said Bienemann.

" 'On Monday, when we went to baseball practice, our lockers were empty. Shan had picked up our suits, even though we were both hitting over .400. That's why I wasn't an eight-letter-winner.'
"Meston grinned.

" 'And that's why I only have one baseball letter,' said the one-time infielder and quarterback, who played *against* Drake for two years before St. Louis dropped football, allowing him to come back home and be immediately eligible at Drake.

SPEECH PROBLEMS

"One reason Meston opted for St. Louis was because of a therapist there who had done good work with speech problems. But no miracles had been performed when Jim returned, still exceedingly sensitive about his problem.

" 'I used to hide out in class, try and sit behind a guy with big shoulders. The best thing that happened was a Drake requirement that everyone take a speech class. When I was a senior, it was pointed out that I never had. So I signed up for a class taught by Hattie Jones. On the first day I was assigned to speak, I skipped class,' he recalls.

" 'The next day, I went to her and explained why I'd done it. She was wonderful. "Why don't you just get up and diagram defenses on the board," she suggested. I did and she got me so confident that the next semester, when I didn't have to, I signed up for speech again.'

"A few years later, in officer's training, Meston discovered that he could arise before a group and be funny. He told about being the quarterback who put 'Hut! Hut! Hut!' into football. 'Before me, it was just "Hut!" ' he'd say. And he'd insist that the Billikens had led the nation in delay of game penalties when he was calling the signals.

" 'Almost anything can be a handicap, but you can accept yourself for what you are,' says Meston, who has written a book, not yet published, on *Building Trust Together*. It's a subject he speaks on often and Chuck Noll, the Steelers' football coach, is so much in agreement with Jim's ideas that he has done the foreword for the book.

RESIDENT HUMORIST

"Meston's work as the resident humorist for the Dapper Dan has brought many friendships with sports figures. Noll, who rarely speaks in public, several times has appeared to talk of motivation before groups put together by Jim.

"Some of his humor is related to sports. 'I had competitive speed,' he tells audiences, of his own career. 'I couldn't beat anybody in the dash. But if someone chased me, they couldn't catch me.' And some of his deliveries aren't sports related.

" 'I travel a lot and was in the same row on a plane as a young man who looked like everything he ate turned to hair,' says Meston. 'I noticed he was wearing one shoe and had one bare foot. As the father of five kids and grandfather of four, I know how to talk to young folks. So I said, 'Hey, man, you lost a shoe.' And he said, 'No, man, like I found a shoe.'

"Somehow, after having breakfast with a guy who has turned a problem into an asset, the idea that man can accomplish almost anything he thinks he can accomplish seems an entirely reasonable assumption."

Chances are *your* speech problems aren't as noticeable as Jim Meston's but his willingness to fight hard to overcome his inhibitions can be a shining example in whatever personal battle you may be having in your attempt to become a better oral communicator.

What is opportunity and when does it knock? Dr. Maxwell Maltz, the famous author and plastic surgeon, said opportunity *never* knocks and that you can wait a lifetime listening and hoping and you will hear no knocking. Rather, he says, "*You are opportunity and you must knock on the door leading to your destiny.*"

CREATIVE OPPORTUNITIES

In his book *The Search for Self-Respect,* Dr. Maltz said: "*You* create opportunity. *You* develop the capacities for moving toward opportunity. *You* turn crises into creative opportunities and defeats into successes and frustration into fulfillment. With what? With your great invisible weapons: your good feelings about yourself, your determination to live the best life you can, and your feeling — that only you can give yourself — that you are a worthwhile, deserving person. You must fight for your right to fulfill the opportunity that God gave you to use your life well."

In a cassette tape that he calls "The Greatest Secret," internationally-known business consultant Joe Batten reminds us that historian Arnold Toynbee said the average age of the world's great civilizations has been 200 years. All nations, Toynbee said, have progressed through the following steps: From bondage to spiritual faith, from spiritual faith to great courage, from courage to liberty, from liberty to abundance, from abundance to selfishness, from selfishness to complacency, from complacency to apathy, from apathy to dependency, from dependency back again to bondage. *But*, said Toynbee, *the most important thing to remember is that our destiny is not predetermined for us — we determine it for ourselves.*

Your destiny and mine can be enhanced, I'm certain, by acceptance of the need, of the importance, of the value of improved oral communications and the shared knowledge that it generates the seeds producing improved human relationships. If you don't believe it, just ask Jim Meston.

Joe Batten will tell you that there are a lot of Jim Mestons in the world — Jim Mestons who indeed determine their own destinies.

If you saw the Academy Award-winning movie Gandhi, I'm sure you were impressed. It all seemed so easy for Gandhi in the film, but life wasn't easy for him. *As a young man he was desperately shy.* He wrote of his youth: "Even when I paid a social call the presence of a half a dozen or more people would strike me dumb."

A REMARKABLE CASE

His biographer, Louis Fischer, said of him: "Gandhi was a self-remade man . . . . It is not that he turned failure into success. Using the clay that was there, he turned himself into another person. He was a remarkable case of a second birth in one lifetime."

In his book *Shyness,* Philip G. Zimbardo of Stanford University says shyness is an insidious personal problem that is reaching such epidemic proportions as to be justifiably called a social disease. He asserts, "Trends in our society suggest it will get worse in the coming years as social forces increase our isolation, competition and loneliness. Unless we begin to do something soon, many of our children and grandchildren will become prisoners of their own shyness. To prevent this, we must begin to understand what shyness is, so that we can provide a supportive environment where shy people can shed the security of their private prisons and regain their lost freedoms of speech, of action, and of human associations."

Adds Zimbardo, "Hawthorne may have been thinking of the shy person when he wrote: 'What other dungeon is so dark/as one's heart? What jailer so inexorable/as one's self?' "

Professor Zimbardo's research indicates that shyness is common, widespread and universal and that in one survey, *more than 80 percent of those questioned reported that they were shy at some point in their lives,* either now, in the past, or always. At the time of his study, he found 40 percent considered themselves **presently** shy — or four out of every ten persons you meet (at least 84 million Americans).

Accompanying shyness, according to Zimbardo, are negative feelings like depression, anxiety and loneliness. Moreover, he says shyness makes it hard to think clearly and communicate effectively.

I believe efforts expended to become a better public speaker will help you greatly if you are a shy person. In one of Zimbardo's surveys, when respondents were asked "What *situation* makes you shy?", the leading response (73%) was, "When I am the focus of attention — in a large group, as when giving a speech."

EVEN MOVIE STARS GET STAGE FRIGHT

One afternoon not long ago I received a long-distance phone call from one of my all-time favorite movie actors — Cary Grant. I was flabbergasted! "Mr. Isaacson," he said, "I just received your letter requesting my comments on how I overcame the fear of public speaking. I wanted you to know that I haven't. Whenever I talk to a large group, my knees rattle so badly I think I should place a board between them to stabilize them."

I couldn't believe it! Here was one of Hollywood's superstars telling me he still gets stage fright. We chatted for a few more minutes, I thanked him profusely for calling, and then hung up. I sat back in my chair and thought, "It's really remarkable. Who would've guessed?"

Outwardly, the Cary Grants of the world don't look the least bit ruffled and that's a good point to remember: **Seldom do we appear as unsettled to the audience as we feel internally.**

Let me cite an example: Sometime ago, I asked several persons at my church to participate in laity day services and to talk to the congregation for five minutes. One of the excellent presentations was made by Gary Davis, who with his wife, Judy, is one of our most active parishioners. Gary told me afterward that he had walked around several blocks before the worship service started to minimize tension and he said that during his talk he was extremely nervous. It didn't show, so again, it's important to remember that those butterflies seldom are obvious to your audience and you shouldn't dwell on it.

ALEC GUINESS SCARED, TOO

England's Alec Guinness, another great film star who has been knighted by his country's queen, likewise confided to me that "I have never got over my fear of speaking in public and do my best to avoid having to speak."

Stage fright, speech fright, fear of public speaking — whatever you choose to call it — is a fear response.

Most observers seem to agree that nervousness caused by public speaking is a result of our feeling that we are in a threatening situation. Our brain triggers a "fight or flee" reaction. Adrenalin is pumped into our bloodstream and causes the heartbeat to race and our blood pressure to rise.

Moreover, our eyes may dilate, our liver may secrete sugar into our blood, digestion may screech to a halt, respiration may speed up and our hair might even stand on end.

Sounds pretty grim, doesn't it? Traumatic, in fact. I'll bet you didn't know that all of that took place just because you got up to speak before a group. Oops, let's add to that: a dry mouth, awkward pauses, quivering, tenseness and fidgeting. That *is* enough to scare your pants off, isn't it?

"But wait a minute," you no doubt are thinking. "Are you saying a beginner can learn how to manage **that?**" My answer is: You bet your bottle of antacid tablets you can do it. Before we talk about ways to manage it, though, let's look at what causes it.

> **EMOTION** — the above-mentioned bodily reactions create an awareness in our minds which in turn helps to create fear.

> **FEAR OF STRANGERS** — it's one thing to chat with a friend at a ballgame or in a line in a supermarket, but we are prone to stand apart and speechless if there are strangers around us.

> **FEAR OF STARING** — most of us don't like being stared at and in a public speaking situation, *we will be stared at.*

> **FEAR OF THE UNUSUAL** — if we aren't used to speaking in public, we have little or no past confidence on which to build. We lack security when faced with an unusual situation.

FEAR OF REJECTION

Cavett Robert maintains that this fear of public speaking actually is basically a fear of *rejection.* We are born with only two fears, says Cavett, and these are the fear of falling and the fear of loud noises. "Speakers think: 'Oh my God. Will I get a standing ovation or will they reject me?' Too often speakers are more concerned with appreciation than with fulfillment and *making a difference in the lives of the audience.*"

He ought to know. Cavett didn't start full-time professional speaking **until he was 60 years of age.** Some 15 years later he is one of the most sought after public speakers in the nation.

How does Cavett recommend managing this fear? "In the first place, speaking is selling. As soon as you can get across the idea that public speaking is *selling your ideas* then I think you will start getting over the fear because you'll start to concentrate on the message and not on yourself.

"I don't want my speech students or salesmen to get rid of this nervousness, this apprehension, this stress. I always said that courage is not getting rid of fear — what would there be to be courageous about if fear wasn't there — courage is learning how to speak, perform and sell in the presence of it. No one ever drowns by falling in the water. You drown if you remain there. No one becomes a good public speaker unless he learns to speak in spite of fear."

Moreover, Cavett says if you have a lackadaisical speaker, you'll have a lackadaisical audience. If you have an exciting speaker, the audience becomes excited. And how does one become an exciting speaker? "You do this by being emotional," says Cavett. "You pay a price for being emotional, however. You don't get something for nothing. It's not good English but it's good philosophy: There ain't no such thing as a free meal."

WE FEAR REJECTION

And what is this price you pay so that you can motivate an audience? Says Cavett, "The price is that you are *sensitive,* you don't like refusal. On the platform the great fear comes that you won't gain *acceptance.* We get that fear of *rejection,* like the little kid who goes to his first dance. He hesitates to ask the pretty girl for a dance because he fears rejection. But I tell my people not to worry about getting rid of this fear of rejection. They can perform effectively in the presence of it."

He believes that if you can handle fear from the platform you can handle fear on a one-to-one basis in other parts of your life. "Everybody can accomplish anything in life they want to," says Cavett, "but so many people are afraid to go out and do things that will accomplish their objectives. They stand in a revolving door and want someone else to push them through. But if you have the passion of a lover, the fire of a crusader, the dedication of a saint, the perseverance of a martyr, if you really *want* something badly enough, that one divine quality will generate and create all the other qualities necessary for success. But nobody can *give* it to you. You don't have to get rid of fear. Just find something that you love enough which has a stronger force than fear."

Never at a loss for a colorful example of a point he's making, Cavett adds, "I love what Napoleon's little drummer boy said: 'I don't know how to beat a retreat and I don't intend to learn!' And if you'll just figure that you'll go ahead regardless, you don't have to worry about fear. And *if you have a message that's crying for expression, you don't have a right not to share it with other people.*"

A KEY CONCEPT

Dr. Eugene F. Gauron of the University of Iowa Department of Psychiatry has received nation-wide attention as a result of his motivational work with athletes, but he tells me the principles that work in athletic endeavor also can be applied to each of us in any walk of life, including public speaking.

A key concept in his work is *"I am what I think I am."* Says Dr. Gauron, "What one thinks and what one says to oneself are critical in terms of what one is able to do. Feelings are affected by thoughts. What one is able to do is affected by thoughts. Changing thoughts changes feelings; changing thoughts liberates other possible behaviors."

He makes another interesting statement, "Many studies investigating differences between elite and non-elite athletes in a variety of sports have shown that self-confidence is a critical factor, *even overriding talent.* The athlete who believes in himself performs at a higher level than a comparable athlete who is lower in self-confidence."

In public speaking, it's obviously important that you believe in yourself and you can take a giant step in that direction by speaking whenever an opportunity presents itself. Frequent exposure to groups will help you gain that needed self-confidence.

THE DALE CARNEGIE METHOD

Dale Carnegie said most fears are actually generated by too much reading, thinking and talking. He believed that we nurse them and feed them until, from an inconsequential trifle, they have grown to monstrous proportions. His suggestion: Repeatedly plunging into the stream of life, adding one conquest to another, overcoming one fear after another until it becomes a habit. He wrote, "We generate fears while we sit; we overcome them by action. Fear is nature's warning signal to get busy."

I know what Carnegie means with regard to too much talking and the power of suggestion. During my formative years, I *never* had any difficulty pronouncing the word "statistic." However, so many people used to tell me what a difficult word it was *for them* to pronounce that even I began faltering over it. In a similar vein, I wonder how many children have a fear of dentistry just because they've heard so many terrible tales about trips to the dentists and the ominous-sounding words "novocaine, drilling, filling, straightening."

Don't YOU be swayed by this negative power of suggestion. And stop to think about it for a moment: **Have you ever seen or heard of a public speaker who collapsed or fainted or otherwise made a terrible fool of himself (unless he were stoned)? I'll bet you haven't, so why place so much credence in some of the scare tactics associated with public speaking?**

United Technologies Corporation offers this food for thought:

DON'T BE AFRAID TO FAIL
> You've failed
> many times
> although you may not
> remember.

You fell down
the first time
you tried to walk.
You almost drowned
the first time
you tried to
swim, didn't you?
Did you hit the ball the
first time
you swung a bat?
Heavy hitters,
the ones who hit the
most home runs,
also strike
out a lot.
R.H. Macy
failed seven
times before his
store in New York
caught on.
English novelist
John Creasey got
753 rejection slips
before he published 564 books.
Babe Ruth struck out
1,330 times,
but he also hit
714 home runs.
Don't worry about
failure.
Worry about the
chance you miss
when you don't
even try.

But you do need to "get busy" working on your own speaking program by developing positive habits, not negative ones. At this point in your reading, I don't want you to think it all looks so dismal. You can have a lot of fun and excitement in the process of improving your public speaking skills and a few laughs, too. For example, I get a tremendous lift just research- ing some of my speech material, especially humorous material. A good friend of mine, who is a clergyman, knew that I was seeking new speech material on this very subject of developing positive habits and he related the following story about the penalty for having *bad* habits:

There were four married couples on their way to Heaven. All had developed bad habits and it was very obvious to St. Peter, who met them at the Pearly Gates.

St. Peter looked at the first man and said, *"You can't come in here now because you're a boozer and all YOU think about is drink, drink, drink. And I notice that even your wife's name is 'Ginny.' "*

St. Peter then looked at the second man and exclaimed, *"You can't come in here now, either, because you are a miser and all YOU think about is money, money, money and I notice that YOUR wife's name is 'Penny.' "*

The third man braced himself and he, too got a negative reaction. *"You can't come in because you worship things that glitter and all you can think about is jewelry, jewelry, jewelry, and I see that YOUR wife's name is 'Ruby.' "*

Hearing all of this, the fourth man turned to his wife and yelled, *"COME ON, FANNIE, HE WON'T LET US IN, EITHER."*

Effective public speaking may not get us a ticket to Heaven, but I like to think that it's a very valuable commodity, nevertheless.

> **"The art of oratory is not dead. It sleeps only when the cause of human freedom sleeps. It is awake and aroused and aware when hope and the ideal are aflame in the hearts of men. Its curse is on idleness, its blessing on work.**
>
> **"It is the protest of faith and courage against despair and cowardice. It is intellectual and emotional dynamite blasting away the rotten and outworn. It demolishes to rebuild. It dares!"**
>
> *Charles Sandburg*

"When you can do the common things of life in an uncommon way, you will command the attention of the world."

GEORGE WASHINGTON CARVER

"Progress involves risk — you can't steal second and keep your foot on first."

UNKNOWN

Life itself can't give you joy,
Unless you really will it;
Life just gives you time and space,
It's up to you to fill it.

UNKNOWN

"He who loses wealth loses much; he who loses a friend loses more; but he that loses his courage loses all."

MIGUEL DE CERVANTES

"Great men think of opportunity, not time. Time is the excuse of feeble and puzzled spirits."

BENJAMIN DISRAELI

He slept beneath the moon,
He basked beneath the sun;
He lived a life of going-to-do,
And died with nothing done.
EPITAPH — JAMES ALBERY

Chapter 4

Here's Additional Reinforcement

"Maybe you think of yourself as a caterpillar when you've really become a butterfly."

Sometimes we become discouraged with our efforts in public speaking. I remember a painfully shy young man who was in my Toastmasters club. He had a tremendous obstacle to climb before he could feel the least bit at ease in a public speaking environment. However, he did make steady progress and the other club members admired him for it. The only problem was HE didn't know he was making progress and HE didn't gain in self-confidence, in spite of the fact that all of his fellow club members encouraged him. He finally quit the club even though personal victory was just around the corner.

There's no denying that the "average" person will experience butterflies and a few shaky moments at the outset, and these usually diminish — both in frequency and in intensity — after a few times a bat.

EVERYONE SPEAKS

Lester Thonssen and Ross Scanlan, whom I mentioned in an earlier chapter, said this about fear, "Everyone speaks, and speaks in order to carry on his social life, whether for pleasure or for profit. Consequently, no one is afraid of 'speaking.' Fear or confusion comes only when we add the word 'public,' for this word suggests such things as a large audience, a momentous occasion, one which makes an unusal demand upon the capabilities of the speaker....'Public speaking' implies for many people a very specialized activity, performed upon very special occasions, and calling for very special talents.

"Right here is the basis for most cases of stage fright. What is more natural than that such a view of the matter should inspire in the individual a profound sense of personal inadequacy? And the probability that he will betray this sense of inadequacy to his public compounds his embarrassment."

How we see ourselves, as in the case of my Toastmaster friend mentioned above, is vitally important to our success or failure. I believe you act according to your *mental image* of things as opposed to the way they really *are*. Remember how scared you used to get when you were a youngster watching a horror movie in a perfectly safe theater?

A COMMON PHENOMENON

Stage fright, it should be emphasized, affects men and women alike, and research studies show that it is unrelated to intelligence, reasoning ability or personality. It is a common phenomenon.

In his book *Public Speaking Without Fear & Trembling*, Mark Hanna makes a couple of very pertinent observations. The first concerns one's audience. Too often we have the feeling that our listeners are going to be terribly hostile. Not so, says Hanna. "The truth is that audiences are not disposed that way. It might be much better if they were. The standard of public speaking would rise. **Audiences are patient, gentle, and infinitely long-suffering.** They have a pathetic hope that the speaker and the speech will be good. This is indeed the triumph of faith over experience. Most audiences are not violent and they do not laugh at the man on the platform. They are sympathetic and eager that he be a success. In view of this, the speaker's task need not be an ordeal at all but an extremely pleasant experience."

CONQUERING FEAR OF SPEAKING

Hanna is very blunt about the subject. "Since stage fright affects all people, what can be done about it? If one is serious about becoming something of a speaker, he might as well say this to himself: 'The first few times I'll be scared stiff. Then the fright will begin to wear off. After that I will begin to have a feeling of ease on the platform, and if I am well prepared, I'll actually enjoy about the fifth or sixth talk.' "

There's nothing to be ashamed of when we experience apprehension during the early stages of our public speaking. After all, G. B. Shaw confessed, "I became a good speaker as other men become good skaters — by making a fool of myself until I got used to it."

Many psychologists believe that a fear learned can be *unlearned.* Moreover, it is universally accepted that facing one's fears is a necessary first step. Psychologist George Weinberg, in his book *Self Creation,* says, "**Any acts of avoidance based on fear will entrench the fear.** This practice . . . is recognized throughout life. Performers of every kind sense its importance. Race-car drivers force themselves to drive again as soon as possible after an accident because otherwise they foresee losing their nerve. Don't let a momentary failure be followed by a lifetime of fear. But avoidance of a situation after a failure can become a way of life. Continuous avoidance can keep the memory of failure fresh in the mind."

FACE FEAR HEAD-ON

Others advise: Face fear head-on, because if you don't, it becomes worse if you fail to identify it and accept it for what it is. Fear and anxiety certainly are prevalent in our society but they can be managed with honest effort.

In a recent issue of *Horizon* magazine, Naomi Graffman wrote a very enlightening article on the impact of stage fright on professional musicians. She writes, "Stage fright — with its awful, sickening lurch in the pit of the stomach; its racing, thumping heart; its clammy hands and shaking knees; its pervasive sense of doom seeping through every pore of the victim's body — does not require a stage to make an appearance. Even the least theatrical among us can be subject to its manifestations. Reliable authorities advise that it's part of the human condition, affecting people in every walk of life; we are told that when our caveman ancestors went out grizzly bear hunting, they, too, suffered from stage fright.

Physiologists describe these unpleasant sensations as the 'fight or flight' reaction and explain that they result from the triggering of the body's defense mechanism, activated by a sudden outpouring of adrenaline. But while this power surge may have helped the caveman in subduing whatever it was that he hoped would become his dinner, its clammy-handed side effects are most emphatically not considered desirable by, say, a concert pianist attempting to cope with a slippery-keyed Steinway."

DRUG NOT A PANACEA

Graffman reports that a relatively new drug — propranolol (commercially known in the United States as Inderal) — is mainly used to treat certain heart conditions, but was said to reduce the symptoms of stage fright without the usual adverse side effects. Users, however, claim that it is not to be considered a panacea and there has been mixed reactions to its effectiveness. One musician, according to Graffman, gave a succinct comment on the fear of public performance: *"There is no escape. The grizzly bear is oneself."*

It should be further noted here that a more recent issue of *Time* magazine also reported the use of this new drug and indicated that some danger exists for people with asthma, hay fever and some types of diabetes and heart conditions.

Personally, I never would use any kind of drug, including alcohol, to give me the courage I needed to speak in public. Many speakers who have participated in a "happy hour" before making their presentations have experienced a mind-numbing situation which had an adverse effect. In other words, self-confidence cannot come from outside oneself. It must be generated from within.

Most of us *know* when duty calls us to do something truly worthwhile. That duty may be right in front of you at this very moment, namely, "Improve thyself!" After all, why do we attend school, go to church, visit the barber, or seek healing if it isn't to improve ourselves?

DON'T IGNORE THE MESSAGE

If it isn't a duty that confronts you, perhaps it's an opportunity that you shouldn't ignore. Take the example of the minister who was preoccupied with writing his sermon. A dam had burst and mountains of water cascaded into the valley where his church stood.

He didn't become aware of the danger until water swirled into his church study. He fled upstairs and looked out the balcony window. A group of people in a boat called out, "Reverend! Reverend! Come with us!" But he shook his head and said, "The Lord will save me."

As the rising water forced him onto the roof, another boat passed by and again the occupants begged him to come along with them. And again he replied, "No, thank you. The Lord will save me."

As he was driven to the top of the bell tower, a third boat passed by, offering assistance. "No, go on," he said. "The Lord will save me."

The water engulfed the church and the next thing the minister knew, he was standing before St. Peter at the Pearly Gates.

"Why, Reverend Jones, " St. Peter said in a surprised voice. "What are YOU doing here?"

"Well, I'm not really sure," the minister replied. "I trusted in the Lord and I thought He would save me from the flood."

St. Peter looked exasperated. "Well," he snapped, "we DID send three boats!"

Have "messages" on the importance of public speaking been sent to you from some source? Your boss? Your customers? Your spouse? Your conscience? If so, why not act now!

A TRUE STORY

Let me tell you another story — a true one — about a man who became a "butterfly" when he could have resigned himself to the lowly position of a caterpillar.

This man struggled against poverty, humiliation, and frequent imprisonment. Born of poor parents, he joined the army as a common soldier and was so severely wounded in battle that he lost the use of his left arm for life.

On his way home, he was captured and held for five years in prison. After his release, he tried to obtain gainful employment but could not, so he re-enlisted in the army in spite of his physical disability. Subsequently he was imprisoned again for indebtedness to his government.

Upon release, he got a job as collector of rents but was persecuted and beaten, and again wound up in prison. In spite of all his misfortune, he maintained an indomitable spirit and wrote one of the all-time best-selling books — *Don Quixote*.

THE BIBLE OF HUMANITY

The author? Miguel De Cervantes, whose masterpiece of literature has been called "the Bible of Humanity." The book still is eagerly read and enjoyed throughout the world some 380 years after it was completed.

The great success of *Don Quixote* becomes even more amazing when it is remembered that at the time it was published, Cervantes had no literary reputation to speak of and was wholly without money or influence. The book had to make its way purely on its own merits.

Don Quixote is rich in humor, humanity and hope. It is a great memorial to the spirit of man.

"Our greatest foes," said Don Quixote, "and whom we must chiefly combat, are within." And one of the most poignant thoughts Quixote expressed bears repeating here: "The world sees people as they are — I see them as they can be!"

Do you see yourself as YOU can be — a confident, dynamic public speaker?

In all fairness to you, it's time for me to put my money where my mouth is and to give you guidelines which I know will work.

SEVEN SURE-FIRE SUCCESS POINTERS

1. Don't necessarily jump in with both feet. Test the speaking water with your toes first, and then submerge more of yourself after you have become accustomed to it. Initially, find subtle opportunities to appear before an audience where you aren't obligated to speak.

   For example, when attending church, a scout meeting or a ballgame, force yourself to proceed to one of the front rows. A good many pairs of eyes will follow you but they'll mostly be seeing your back. During a lull in activities, get up, and walk out to get a drink of water or to go to the restroom. Again, people will be looking at you but so what.

   When crossing a busy street on a green light, dare to look at the drivers of the stopped cars. It's almost a staring-back situation but it will help you gain more self-confidence.

   I've found another good method for initial ice breaking is to actually volunteer to be an usher at public functions. I used to usher at my church, at our city's civic center, and at other events where I knew I would be in front of a crowd.

2. Volunteer to make calls for religious or other charitable organizations, such as the United Way, Junior Achievement or Community Blood Bank. Often you'll receive rejections (a parishioner doesn't want to make a pledge or a company president decides not to give this year to your community organizations). But you will gain valuable experience in trying to sell a worthwhile cause and you'll begin to toughen your thin skin.

3. Contact the leadership of the organizations you belong to and volunteer to be the treasurer or recording secretary. This means you'll have to read the treasurer's report or the minutes at the next meeting. And when you do, don't read them sitting down. Stand up and as you're reading, look up occasionally at your audience. In many organizations, particularly those of a religious nature, an opening prayer and devotions are appropriate and you could volunteer to handle these functions, too. And while you have the floor, make additional comments about the organization, its objectives, your job in it, its capable officers and how pleased you are to be a part of it.

4. While shopping, find an excuse to ask a clerk or a department manager for special information or directions. This will reinforce your ability to deal with strangers. Or, if you've received especially good and polite service, give the clerk a 60-second compliment and tell him or her you'll look forward to shopping there again.
   Make a friendly comment to other passengers on public elevators.

5. Force yourself to make a round of introductions when a newcomer joins your social group. Or when a new employee joins your company, volunteer to take him or her around to the various departments for introductions.

6. Widen your circle of participation as you gain a little more confidence. Join your church choir, ask for a small part in your community drama group, be a Sunday school teacher, a Boy Scout or Girl Scout leader, a Parent-Teacher Association officer. The important thing is *to do something in the way of group oral communication on a regular basis.*

One of my sons volunteered for telephone duty at Crisis Line, a division of our local United Way office. He received group training — resulting in his participation in a number of group discussions, which helped to develop his self-confidence. Moreover, he performs a very valuable community function by helping troubled callers with their personal problems, some of which are quite debilitating.

Participation in neighborhood political caucuses is another method for making oneself a participant instead of a bystander.

7. As your confidence increases, it now may be time for you to enroll in an adult education speech course (see chapter 7 for additional information on public speaking programs offered). Never forget that every journey consists of a series of steps. Begin your speaking journey now! Some of the following quotations may help you.

> "There is no trick in learning to speak courageously, confidently and persuasively. The real trick is ever getting a person to embrace the sincere desire, that deep compulsion within himself, to speak. Yes, getting it within himself. When this is once accomplished, then success in speaking will follow in natural sequence . . . The law of hard work and constant effort can surely make you a good speaker."
>
> CAVETT ROBERT

> "I have no doubt whatever that most people live, whether physically, intellectually or morally, in a very restricted circle of their potential being . . . . we all have reservoirs of life to draw upon of which we do not dream."
>
> WILLIAM JAMES

> "I prayed to the Lord, and he answered me; he freed me from all my fears."
>
> PSALMS 34:4

> "If you don't have the power to change yourself, then nothing will change around you."
>
> ANWAR SADAT

> "When we know who and what we wish to be, we will find it relatively easy to know what to do."
>
> JOE BATTEN

"I am behind the wheel in my life. Losers let it happen — winners make it happen."
                    DR. DENIS E. WAITLEY

"Maybe you think of yourself as a caterpillar when you've really become a butterfly!"
                    JEAN M. CIVIKLY

"Jesus came preaching — not writing. It is one of the amazing things in history."
                    A. IAN BURNETT

"Do you *really* enjoy watching a football game, a baseball game, or a tennis match? Or would you rather be crossing the goal line, hitting the home run, or getting the ace yourself? The fact that you are only watching means that you either cannot or do not want to be a performer. Yet somehow you derive vicarious joy. Perhaps you know that you could outperform them if only . . . "
                    RICHARD S. SLOM

"Probably 98% of what we call anxiety crops up as *overconcern for what someone thinks about you...* If you fear that you speak poorly, vigorous focusing on the content of your talk rather than on the reactions of your audience will often calm your fears."
                    ALBERT ELLIS, Ph.D.
          and   ROBERT A. HARPER, Ph.D.

"Too many of us waste our years waiting for better times in the future or wondering about better times in the past, instead of working for better times in the present. If only we had lived in better times or had been born in better times! If only we lived with better people or belonged to a less underprivileged and despised group! If only we lived in a better home or a better town! If only we had a better business or a better job! If—if—if! Tomorrow—tomorrow— tomorrow! But today is always here; yesterday is gone, and tomorrow may never come. No, now is the time—here is the place. This is the person. This is your home. This is your job. This is your wife—your husband—your child—your mother—your friend. This is your people. This is your country. This is your generation. You can have a wonderful time just where you are, just when you are, just how you are, just with whomever you are."

DR. LOUIS BINSTOCK

"Winning individuals do not leave the development of their potential to chance, they pursue it systematically and look forward to an endless dialogue between their potentialities and the claims of life — not only claims they encounter but the claims they invent."

JOHN GARDNER

"Be human. Admit your weaknesses. Then bury them!"

J.V. CERNEY

The Art Of Persuasion

The other night I attended a dinner party where our hostess was a lively, imaginative lady. "Tell me," she asked her guests at one point, "if you suddenly discovered you had a fairy godmother willing to grant you one gift — *just one* — to improve your personality, what would you ask for?"

No two people had the same idea. One guest said he would wish for a sharper sense of humor. Another said she would request liberation from her inferiority complex. A third thought for what seemed like a full minute. Finally he said, "I'd ask for *the gift of persuasion.*It's not only the most useful skill in the world, it's the most rewarding. It's fun!"

I've been pondering those words and I believe that man was right. Successful persuasion *is* fun. Not only that, it is absolutely essential to successful living in our times.

Just look around you. In any profession, any enterprise, the man or woman at the top is almost always a master persuader. The rank and file use it constantly, too. Every time I preach a sermon I'm trying to persuade people to buy a certain thought pattern. We're *all* persuaders, *every one of us.*

DR. NORMAN VINCENT PEALE

Chapter 5

How Famous Persons Cope

"It's spit-up time."

Earlier in the book, I mentioned my conversation with actor **Cary Grant** and commented that he never got over his fear of public speaking. He told me, "If I do have to speak somewhere, I'm nervous for two weeks ahead of time. I say to myself, 'Oh, God, why do I do this to myself?' "

But he went on to tell me — and I think this is the key thing to remember for *all* public speakers — that a speaker needs to know what really *interests* an audience. Then, the speaker is more at ease and the audience receives greater benefit from the presentation.

Earl Nightingale makes the same point. He says emphatically, "The cardinal sin in making speeches is to be *uninteresting!*"

The phenomenal **Dr. Norman Vincent Peale** is another luminary who still suffers from stage fright. He has written close to 30 books, given thousands of sermons and public lectures but still has butterflies.

TREMORS OF FEAR

He told me, "As to your question how I overcame the fear of public speaking, the answer is that I have never fully overcome it. As I hear myself being introduced to a large audience I begin to feel tremors of fear. As a boy I was extremely shy, and it clings to my mind even yet. I overcome it by getting myself out of the center of my thoughts, and instead, thinking of those I might help. I pray and ask the Lord to help me, then believing that He will, I step forward and start talking. Then the fear leaves me, and I feel free and relaxed."

He continued, "Your second question is, 'How have you handled fear in other parts of your life?' The answer is that fear is a thought pattern, and any thought pattern can be changed by a process of displacement. The only thing greater than fear is faith. So therefore I endeavor to keep my mind full of faith; faith in God and faith in myself as a child of God. I find that the more faith I have the less fear I have."

When asked by another interviewer, "Does your nervousness disappear as you face a crowd or do you still have to overcome an uneasy feeling?" **Oral Roberts** replied, "I think that I have always felt a certain amount of nervousness before any sermon. If I don't feel enough, I'm in trouble. If I feel too much, I'm in trouble. But, you have to feel a certain amount, but certainly when I know the anointing is upon me, I know I am adequate."

IN CONTROL

He continued, "I suppose that is the greatest support that is given to me — I am adequate to preach this sermon. I'm in control of this situation. And there was a time in my ministry prior to that that I couldn't say that and the anointing plus the preparation, of course, that'll cure a lot of headaches."

He adds, "Fear is a reverse form of faith. Fear is almost like faith, it's just believing in the wrong thing. It's having faith, not in God, and not in abundant life, not in the good things, but having faith in something that you don't want to happen . . . God says He didn't give it to you, or give it to me."

In one of his publications he tells of a boyhood experience: "When I was a boy I was always afraid of dogs. When I would see a dog coming, I would run as fast as I could. I had a newspaper route in Atoka, Oklahoma, and one house had a dog that had run me off every day for a month. One evening as I approached that house, I said to myself, 'I'm not going to run. I'm *not* going to be afraid.'

"I got within about 50 feet of the house, and here came that dog, barking his head off, running pell-mell toward me. I stood perfectly still. The dog ran right up to me and slid up to my shins. I didn't move. I just stared at him. That old dog looked at me, took one sniff, turned and ran off! Many times since, I have said that other fears are like that dog."

PREPARATION BUILDS CONFIDENCE

Does a former professional football player, now a famous coach, know fear of public speaking? Here's what **Tom Landry** of the Dallas Cowboys told me: "I have been able to overcome my fear of public speaking through proper preparation of the subject that I am speaking on. Public speaking is really not something that came easy for me, especially in the beginning. I have had to spend a great deal of time in preparing the material that I wanted to present and quite a bit of time rehearsing. I believe that if you do these two things then you will be able to handle yourself before a crowd. Someone once said that it takes 30 minutes of preparation for each minute that you are before a crowd. I believe that this is true.

"My Christian faith has made a great difference to me in

handling fear in my life. Second Timothy 1:7 states that God does not give us a spirit of fear, but He gives us power, love and self-control. This is how I face all situations where fear is present. It is much easier to handle fear when one realizes that fear does not come from God."

Zig Ziglar, no doubt one of the outstanding speakers and motivators of our time, told me that fear of public speaking really never had a chance to get a firm grip on him. He said, "As far as fear is concerned, I was the tenth of 12 children so I got here with an audience to speak to, and fear seemed not to be too big a factor. As a salesman, at an early age I started conducting group demonstrations of from two to 10 couples, and while this was public speaking, since I had a product to demonstrate and something to hold in my hands and talk about, I was not subjected perhaps to the 'normal' fears to which most public speakers are subjected.

STARTED SALES ORGANIZATION

"From there I started a sales organization and my first sales meeting was between another salesman and myself. I gradually grew to an organization of well over 100, but again the growth was gradual and to a large degree little or no fear was involved. The third phase involved the selling of tickets to come to a major seminar to hear Dr. Kenneth McFarland, Elmer Wheeler, Joe Batten, Senator Milward Simpson, and Charles Roth do the speaking. Those speeches involved anywhere from 10 to 250 so the transition into speaking to large groups was so gradual that I escaped most of the natural fears that speakers normally deal with.

"For a long time I have felt only excitement in facing an audience, and gratitude for the privilege. Fear is not a part of my performance.

"Fear in the other parts of my life has been minimal, though I suppose that an underlying fear which I had for years would be the fear of failure and the fear that I would not be able to accomplish some of the things which I had hoped to accomplish. On July 4, 1972, I committed my life to Christ and I do not recall any major fears since then. Obviously, all of us are plagued with an occasional doubt, but I really would separate that from fear, inasmuch as I lost no sleep over it and thus far have missed no meals because of it. God bless you in your efforts."

START AT EARLY AGE

Another former professional football star, now a respected national TV figure, is **Merlin J. Olsen**. Yes, this hulk of a man does continue to experience nervousness before a presentation. He said, "Max, the best way I know of to get over the fear of speaking is to start at an early age and to do it as often as possible. My mom got me started at age 6. She was a former teacher and helped me memorize speeches for church and school at a very early age.

"I still get nervous before I speak but I'd be concerned if that did not happen. The energy and the excitement would not be there without that rush of adrenaline. The key for me today is to make sure I am totally and completely prepared, and that I have a message of value and interest for my audience.

"Fear is one of the silent motivators in our lives. Fear of failure spurs us to perform, but is often less frustrating than our fear of success. Learning how to deal with fear by facing up to it, confronting it, is essential to our well being and our comfort level.

"Our first reaction is to run from fear, to ignore it — to push it back into the darkness. If we do that, those fears grow and multiply and can become debilitating.

"On the other hand, if we stand toe to toe with those things that frighten us, examining them, turning them over so they can be seen from all angles, we often find that they are not so scary after all. It's also helpful to be able to admit to ourselves and others that there are things we're afraid of."

JUST BE YOURSELF

In her inimitable way, syndicated columnist **Erma Bombeck** related how she feels about the subject: "If you have a cure for walking out on a stage looking over a sea of several hundred faces in the clutches of deep depression and trying to deliver a first line, I would love to know what it is. I have never gotten over the phobia of public speaking. Every lecture is spit-up time.

"There is probably only one thing that has kept me going. My baptism on a talk show was in 1967. It was the Tonight Show hosted by Johnny Carson in New York. About an hour before I was to go on, my mother (who occasionally traveled with me) said to me, 'If you are going out there and try to be something you're not, you have every reason in this world to be terrified. If you're going to go out there and be honest and do the best you can, it's a piece of cake.' That single speech has probably sustained me more often than she knew.

"One of the hardest parts of delivering a humorous speech is the patience to wait out the audience. Don't panic and let them come to you. It takes an uncommon amount of guts."

Vivacious former Miss America **Marilyn Van Derbur** currently operates a very successful motivational institute in Denver. How scared did she get? Consider this, "Fear would not adequately describe how I felt about speaking in public — terror would be a more accurate word! I did not seek the Miss America title . . . I knew after having been selected Miss University of Colorado that it would require speaking in public so I enrolled in a summer course at our Opportunity School here in Denver.

TERRIFIED

"Our first assignment was to recite a short poem or reading. I was totally prepared but when my boyfriend was driving me to class and asked me to recite what I was going to do in class and I did, he laughed. He would never have meant to hurt my feelings. He just had no understanding of how terrified I was to stand up in front of a group of people. That took away the confidence I had mustered and I never did go to that class. Instead, within five weeks I was facing 25,000 people in Atlantic City and 85,000,000 on television.

"I have addressed an average of 10,000 people a week for 20

years and at least 15 of those years I had stage fright before every speech. It has only been in recent years after having more than paid my dues, that I have become not only comfortable but find speaking to be an extremely easy and joyful experience.

"One way I overcame my fear was to believe so strongly in what I was saying that my goal of reaching individual people became more important than my fear. I truly did find something 'larger than myself.'

"In addition, I spent hours going over and over and over my materials so that I knew it backwards, forwards and upside down. I was, in every instance, totally and completely prepared. I have never been afraid to risk failure. I have put my life on the line many, many times and for reasons I'm not sure I understand have never backed away from a challenge that was important to me.

DECLINED THE INVITATION

"In other areas of my life when I have been asked to do things that I did not feel comfortable doing and knew that 'fear' would be ever present, I declined the invitation. It was, for many years, an endless battle but it has been well worth it and I hope I would not be arrogant in saying that I feel I have touched, in a very personal and meaningful way, many lives. Perhaps this is what kept me going!!"

Another outstanding woman of our times is former Congresswoman and U.S. Senator **Margaret Chase Smith**. She writes, "Never having been trained for speaking, I learned whatever I did by way of experience. In other words, I never tried to be an orator, my objective being to get my story across to my listeners in simple and sincere language with brevity. In any effort I ever made I did the best that I could, never with fear but always with confidence and determination."

One of the Wizard of Oz stars and a fascinating member of the entertainment world is actor/dancer/movie star **Ray Bolger**. He told me, "My fear of 'public speaking' has a twist. My business (show business) caused me to appear in front of vast numbers of peoples, to talk, sing, dance, make them laugh, etc. Yet if I had to make a serious speech (or I might put it this way — a non-performance speech) I feared I was not equipped vocabulary-wise.

"So I did something about it. I took a course on speech, phonetics and reading aloud at Columbia University. Then I went out and hunted for opportunities to speak — on any subject. This caused me to do research, write and deliver. It worked.

"In the other parts of my life, I handled fear the same way. I face the problem and solve it by not letting the fear of trying keep me from *licking* that problem. Once I had claustrophobia. I no longer have it."

TIPS FROM AN AWARD WINNING SPEAKER

For years, one of the most prominent names in the business world has been the name of **Joe Batten**, highly successful management consultant, training professional and film producer. He also has earned the CPAE award, the highest in the National Speakers Association. Joe is headquartered in my home town of Des Moines and he and I occasionally cross paths. I recently asked him how he has handled fear in his life. Here's what the author of the all-time best-selling management book, *Tough Minded Management*, told me how he controlled *his* fear of public speaking.

"The answer here can be summarized in the word **confrontation**. I really didn't feel I had a choice because the requests to speak poured in after my first book was published and I felt an obligation to my colleagues as President of the company to meet these requests for economic reasons. This was compounded by the residuals of a speech impediment.

"It helped a great deal to speak on a subject I had written a book about — I felt **prepared**. Nevertheless, I would perspire until my shirt was wet. I kept laboring and slugging away — and my fear remained. Then, I began to discover the thrill of sharing ideas with audiences that would enrich there lives — and — the **implosive** tensions turned into **explosive** tensions.

My fears evaporated when I began to experience a feeling of **giving, transmitting,** and **projecting**. In short, when the desire to **get** was transformed into a desire to **give,** the fears were gone.

VALUE SYSTEM

"Sounds simple, doesn't it? And — it is, but simple things are often tougher to do with excellence than complex things. Since then, I have written many books, made numerous films and tapes, and they provide the value system, the insights, needed to carry out a life-style based on giving.

"How have I handled fear in other parts of my life? These fears run the gamut from fear of death on Guadalcanal in the Marine Corps to fear that a child will be kicked by a horse. I guess I'd recommend the same recipe as above for all of these. As long as we live within a constricted web of 'defensive' thoughts, we'll find ample bases for rationalizing those defenses by constantly perceiving 'fearsome' elements in every dimension of life.

"It is important to augment a commitment to a giving life-style by learning to **enjoy the challenge of being vulnerable.** Learn to literally seek out and relish obstacles and difficulties which **test** you. Then — they won't **threaten** you."

Og Mandino has written numerous best-sellers and has millions of admiring readers. His book *The Greatest Salesman In The World* is a run-away success. Og is as sincere as his writing and is one of the most considerate "famous people" I've ever met. The last time I saw him at a speakers convention, he was sharing his experience on writing and publishing with an admiring audience.

Earlier, he had responded promptly and succinctly to my query about fear.

A LITTLE EASIER EACH TIME

"My **first** speech, in 1974, was to close a success rally on which had appeared Larry Wilson, Earl Nightingale and W. Clement Stone ahead of me. I was too dumb to be frightened. By the time I gave my second speech I was terrified. The fear

just gradually subsided a little more each time I walked out on
the platform and after about twenty or so most of it had been
overcome just by the sheer doing. Now, after about six
hundred or so, the closest thing to fear shows up about two
hours before I'm scheduled to be 'on' and it hits me in my hotel
room. A 'little man' inside me starts asking questions like,
'What are you doing here?' 'You don't need this fee, why aren't
you back in Scottsdale playing golf?' etc. etc. But that all goes
away and I truly enjoy myself while I'm doing my thing —
perhaps because the audiences are so receptive since, thank
God, there's always a good percentage of them who have read
one or more of my books.

"The last time I can actually remember real **fear** was back in
the days when I was flying combat as a bombardier in the
Eighth Air Force, over Germany. I just did what my mother
taught me when I was a kid. I prayed a lot. I still do.

"I have a tough time overcoming inertia and lethargy. I am
blessed with more material assets than I can ever possibly
spend so that if I never write another word or give another
speech, neither I nor my family will ever go hungry. This fact,
pleasant as it is, makes it tough to get cranked up and motivated. Pride eventually comes to the rescue. Whether I'm
working on a new book, or delivering a speech, I just can't let
those people down who have been exposed to my words and
expect superhuman things from me. I fail, often, I'm sure, but I
sure try like hell . . . because I don't want to let them down . . .
and I refuse to let me down."

DEEP INFERIORITY COMPLEX

Writer/poet/philosopher **Rod McKuen's** admirers are
legion, too. His written comments to me are almost poignant
when he discusses life, death and obligations. He says, "I can
honestly never remember being afraid to speak in public,
whether in a poolroom or at the podium. That probably says a
great deal about the amount of ham in me. I've always had a
deep inferiority complex but that probably stems from physical abuse I received as a child. Somewhere along the way, I
learned to disguise some of my defects by putting on the coat of

an extrovert. My friends moan about the fact that I am still very introverted and shy. I admit to being a hermit, but I would honestly rather stay at home than go out just to be going out.

"One thing I do believe very strongly as a performer and lecturer; there is no such thing as a bad audience. I might at times give a bad performance, or on occasion be guilty of being a bad performer, but whether I'm appearing before 2, 200 or 225,000 people, I believe the audience is made up of the same percentage of people who say 'Show Me' as there are those who have come to really root for me. Some have headaches, heartburn, have had a quarrel with a husband or wife, or are just checking me out for the first time. The audience pays its money and it takes its chances. If at the end of a concert, the crowd isn't on its feet cheering, I stumbled somewhere during the performance and failed to keep the people's interest. It's always my fault, not theirs.

"I'm surprised that the phobia surrounding Public Speaking is at the top of the list of those things we all agonize over. I don't even believe in the so-called 'Silent Majority' that Spiro T. Agnew consistently referred to in his public life. Any majority that isn't talking or bitching or edifying, lives beneath those marble forests some call graveyards.

DEPRESSION HAS ITS PLACE

"How have I handled fear in other parts of my life? Even as a child, when my stepfather would beat me for no apparent reason, I don't think I was afraid. Stage Fright? No. Fear of earthquakes, fire, famine? No really. Although I'm aware that pestilence, purgatory and perdition sometimes wait in the wings, I really look upon them as something I don't have much control over and to be afraid of the dark is to fear the light.

"Only in the dark parts of the mind, do we learn to make our fantasies come true. Only through blackness do we appreciate light. Even depression has its place in life because if we have any feeling about survival at all, it forces us to work.

"I suppose as I grow older, I'm beginning to fear the end a little bit. Not death itself, since I believe that from the moment we are born, we continuously move towards death, but I am genuinely afraid that death may sneak up on me before I find out completely what God expects of me in life. I can't believe that I am on this planet merely to take up space. I also believe that nobody, not my country, family, friends, anyone, owes me anything. If I were to spend the rest of my life trying to pay back all the good things that have happened to me, I couldn't possibly finish the job. Now that I'm on to the debt I owe, I'm trying, but it seems too little and I can't believe I will ever reach a state where I know it will be enough.

"I hope that I haven't skirted your questions, but I'm convinced that fear is not so much a phobia as it is an excuse we often use for our own unwillingness to **try**."

ADVICE FROM A COLUMNIST

Reports from journalists produced a variety of statements with regard to the fear of public speaking. **Ann Landers** told me, "I am one of the fortunate few who never experienced stage fright. From the earliest days of platform appearances, I was confident and fear-free because I felt that I knew my subject well and could handle any kind of question. I have feared very few things in my life. As a child I prayed for God's protection when I felt I needed it and He never let me down."

James J. Kilpatrick seemed equally confident when he wrote, "I doubt that I can be of much help to you. I began making speeches about 1950, when I was editor of the *Richmond (Va.) News Leader.* Local custom decreed that the editor was expected to talk occasionally to the local Rotarians, Kiwanians, Lions, Optimists, and others. I suppose I suffered some brief and transient qualms, but I truly can't recall any 'fear' of public speaking. H.L. Mencken once wrote of the latent tendency in many men 'to strut and roll their eyes,' and I reckon I had more than my share of that tendency."

One of my favorite TV personalities, **Hugh Downs** of ABC News, explains his technique for handling fear of public speaking. "It didn't happen instantly, but I gradually shifted my concern from how I looked and sounded, to what I was saying. Somehow when you give full attention to subject matter and audience, you wind up looking and sounding better than when you're focused on yourself.

"My technique for handling fear in other parts of my life has been to behave as though nothing fearsome is at hand. I suppose this has a slight flavor of the ostrich, but I found that if I force myself to remain cool, fear never gets a grip on me. Joe Garagiola used to call me 'Charlie Cool' implying that courage was a factor in this image. I had to explain to him that the truth is more likely that I fail to realize fully the depth of danger until the crisis has passed. This gives a marvelous illusion of bravery."

A FEW MINUTES WITH ANDY ROONEY

I get a big kick out of watching **Andy Rooney** on the top-rated TV production "60 Minutes" and also find his syndicated column very entertaining. He reflects still another viewpoint.

He writes, "Your question assumes I've overcome my fear of public speaking and I have not. I dread it whether I'm speaking in front of 2,500 people in a convention hall or the fifth grade class in my local public school.

"I have not handled fear very well in other parts of my life, either. With the exceptions of public speaking and death, there aren't many things I'm afraid of."

In a recent syndicated column in the *Des Moines Register*, he holds forth in greater detail:

> "If you've ever talked in front of a group of more than 10 people, you know how nervous you get. In the past few years, I've spoken about 20 times to large audiences, and I was as nervous before the last one as I was before the first.
>
> There are some things I've learned and some observations I've made about speechmaking:
>
> • Sitting at the head table, waiting for your turn while everyone eats dinner for several hours, is the hardest part of making a speech at a banquet.

• A lot of organizations that ask you to speak don't really care what you talk about as long as you show up on time and don't talk for too long.

• You have to give a longer speech when the event is held in an auditorium than you do when you're speaking at a dinner, because in an auditorium those people came for the single purpose of hearing you.

• If you make a half-hour speech, it takes about three weeks. It takes a day to get there, a day to get back, a couple of days to prepare it and several weeks to worry about it.

• It's strange to be 'introduced' by someone you never met.

• Getting dressed in a hotel room before a speech, I almost always find there's something wrong with my clothes. There's a button missing on my shirt, I brought brown socks and I'm wearing a blue suit, or there's a spot on my necktie.

• The strange thing about speaking is that you only know for sure that you've made a point with an audience when you say something funny and they laugh. If you make what you hope is a good, serious point, there's no way for them to let you know.

• No matter how bad I may have been, someone always comes up to me and tells me I was great. If most people are polite and distant when you're leaving, you know you bombed out as a speaker.

• Someone always thanks you profusely for coming even when they've paid you to do it.

• There are few pleasanter times in life than when you've finished speaking."

"Never rise to speak till you have something to say; and when you have said it, cease."

COOLIDGE

Chapter 6

A Program For Realizing Your Goals

"After you get where you're going — where will you be?"

"Not long ago there was a basketball game between two rival college teams. The score, with only seconds left on the clock, was Virginia Tech 77, Florida State 77. Florida State missed a shot. The rebound was grabbed by a 6-foot 5-inch Virginia Tech forward named Les Henson. With one second on the clock, he threw the ball 89 feet and 3 inches across the entire court. Swish! Right into the basket.

"The place erupted in pandemonium. The coach was on the floor, incoherent. The players jumped on top of the coach.

Everybody from Virginia Tech was having a great time, excited and enthusiastic, except Les, who sat quietly on the bench. The press came up to him and asked if he knew what he had done.

" 'Les, you've set a collegiate record! The longest field goal in the history of collegiate basketball! Why aren't you going crazy like everybody else?'

"Do you know what his answer was? *'That's where I was aiming!'* "

WHAT'S YOUR GOAL?

"Are you aiming high enough?" That's what Jack Wilmer, director of marketing and sales training for Wrangler Brand/Blue Bell Inc., asks his salespeople when he shares with them the Les Henson story. That's a good question to ask you — the reader — in your goal-setting as a public speaker. Are YOU aiming high enough?

Perhaps you have had the feeling that you're going nowhere—and have already arrived. Have you been frustrated in your attempts to reach a certain objective in your personal or business life? Have you ever thought *"Boy, if only I had a million dollars my worries would be over"?*

I can answer "yes" to the above. We seek luck, good fortune, the breaks in life because most of us have problems of one kind or another—real or imagined. Ironically, though, some of the most stable people in our society are those who are poor. Some of the most unstable are those with wealth. Now, you're probably thinking that you'd sure like to have a stab at being a millionaire; like the pauper who said, "give me the luxuries of life and I will gladly do without the necessities."

SOMETHING IS WRONG

Today, we exist in an age of gross materialism. It's a paradox—the more we have physically the less it seems we are happy emotionally and mentally. People have the feeling that something is wrong but they can't put their finger on the cause of their emptiness.

What can we do to dispel the feeling of emptiness? I think that in the long run it might be well for us to have a goal that is beyond our reach, because it's in the reaching that we find ourselves the healthiest emotionally. Too often a conquest, a goal *reached* leaves us feeling a little hollow and unchallenged.

It might best be stated, then, that a program for realizing your goals is one which encourages you to work diligently for a degree of excellence that is unreachable. In the process, though, a high degree of accomplishment can be the result.

Why reach in the first place? What stimuli are there which can prod us into goal-seeking? Consider the part of the *Talmud* which says, "Every man has the right to feel that 'because of me was the world created.' "

If an individual can feel such deep self-esteem then he or she is bound to face life with confidence and expectancy. In life we must enjoy all of God's gifts no matter what. That doesn't mean that we should be arrogant — or as cocky and head-strong as Charles DeGaulle, who allegedly called the Vatican to inquire about the possibility of being buried in the Holy Sepulchre. *"Yes, you can be buried there,"* replied the Vatican, *"but it will cost you $100,000,000."* And DeGaulle replied, in amazement, *"What, $100,000,000 for only three days???"*

DEFINING SUCCESS

A long time ago I read (and agreed with) one philosopher's view of life and I apologize for failing to remember who it was. Anyway, he said something to the effect that there are three broad areas of success for the average individual. First is the satisfaction coming from the continued mutual sharing of love, affection and fellowship with family and friends.

A second major area for success in life—and one that is often put first—is the area of business, career and financial success. This, of course, involves much more than making money. For the intelligent person, his interest in and satisfaction from the building of successful career or business is one of the high points of life.

The third area of life in which success should be achieved is the personal and spiritual sphere. Why we are here, where we are going—whether to excel or not and in what direction—are basic questions needing to be understood for true success in the personal and spiritual aspects of everyone's life.

And whether we want to excel with our personal communications—in particular our **oral** communications, our public speaking—is an individual choice. No one but you can do it. As Dr. Kenneth Hildebrand noted sometime ago in an issue of *Success* magazine:

> ". . . struggle calls forth achievement and forms character. Solid character is not inherited from our father or mother, or from illustrious ancestors. A sturdy character is not created by easy circumstances. Character is the fruit of our own individual endeavors—how we react to the raw occurrences of life. Character is the reward of moral courage, right thinking and honorable action, the fruit of hope, endurance and patience. If we dedicate ourselves to easy defeat and frustration, if we form the habit of running away from frowning situations, nothing can prevent us from becoming miserable and unhappy weaklings.

> "When tempted to run away, you must call on your resolution, not your doubts and fears. You sharpen your abilities only when you encounter something difficult and battle against it with determination and courage. You never get your second wind except in the long race. You never learn to swim in the shallow pools. You never learn to play tennis with the net down. You never gain sturdiness if you quit before reaching the top of the first steep hill, and the one after that."

THE FIRST KEY — PERSEVERANCE

Yes, if we are to reach our objective of becoming a better public speaker, one of the first keys of success is PERSEVERANCE. I've always enjoyed the story about the sales convention where the corporate sales manager got up in front of his firm's 2,000 salespersons and said, "Did the Wright Brothers ever quit?" The sales force shouted: "NO!" He yelled, "Did Charles Lindbergh every quit?" Again the sales people shouted: "NO!" He yelled a third time, "Did Billy Martin every quit?" Again the sales people shouted: "NO!" "Did Thorndike McKeester ever quit?"

There was a long silence. Finally, one lone man stood up and asked, "Who's Thorndike McKeester? We never heard of him." And the sales manager snapped back, "Of course you never heard of him, because HE quit!"

THE SECOND KEY — THE WISE USE OF TIME

The second key is THE WISE USE OF TIME. It's so easy to procrastinate . . . to put off until tomorrow what we should be doing today. So many people postpone truly important things in life. Here's a poignant piece on the subject of puttings things off:

The Station
By Robert J. Hastings

Tucked away in our subconscious minds is a vision — an idyllic vision — in which we see ourselves on a long journey that spans an entire continent. We're traveling by train and, from the windows, we drink in the passing scenes of cars on nearby highways, of children waving at crossings, of cattle grazing in distant pastures, of smoke pouring from power plants, of row upon row upon row of cotton and corn and wheat, of flatlands and valleys, of city skylines and village halls.

But uppermost in our conscious minds is our final destination — for at a certain hour and on a given day, our train will pull into the station with bells ringing, flags waving, and bands playing. And once that day comes, so many wonderful dreams will come true, and all the jagged pieces of our lives will fit together like a completed jigsaw puzzle. So, restlessly, we pace the aisles and count the miles, peering ahead, cursing the minutes for loitering, waiting,

waiting, waiting for the station . . . .

"Yes, when we reach the station, that will be it!" we cry. "When we're eighteen! When we buy that new 450 SL Mercedes Benz! When we put the last kid through college! When we win that promotion! When we pay off the mortgage! When we retire!" Yes, from that day on, like the heroes and heroines of a child's fairy tale, we will all live happily ever after.

Sooner or later, however, we must realize there is no station, no one place to arrive at once and for all. The journey is the joy. The station is an illusion — it constantly outdistances us. Yesterday's a memory; tomorrow's a dream. Yesterday belongs to history; tomorrow belongs to God. Yesterday's a fading sunset; tomorrow's a faint sunrise. So, shut the door on yesterday and throw the key away, for only today is there light enough to live and love. It isn't the burdens of today that drive men mad. Rather, it's regret over yesterday and fear of tomorrow. Regret and fear are twin thieves who would rob us of that Golden Treasure we call today, this tiny strip of light between two nights.

"Relish the moment" is a good motto, especially when coupled with Psalm 118:24: "This is the day which the Lord hath made; we will rejoice and be glad in it."

So stop pacing the aisles and counting the miles. Instead, swim more rivers, climb more mountains, kiss more babies, count more stars. Laugh more and cry less. Go barefoot oftener. Eat more ice cream. Ride more merry-go-rounds. Watch more sunsets. Life must be lived as we go along. The station will come soon enough.

THE THIRD KEY — AVOID DISCOURAGEMENT

Almost everyone has a bad day now and then, but if you

string too many of them together, serious depression can set in. If you hope to achieve your goals in public speaking, you must be careful to AVOID DISCOURAGEMENT. That's the third key.

I've always found light at the end of the tunnel. There have been dark days in my business, in my investments, and in my public speaking, but I've tried hard not to succumb to discouragement. More than once I've given a speech that seemed to fall flat and afterward I would say to myself: "Why bother to speak in public again?"

Invariably, though, my next speech turns out to be a barn-burner and I'm always thankful I didn't quit.

Edmund Burke, the great British statesman, said, "Never despair, but if you do, **work on in despair.**"

The name Henry Francis Lyte may not ring a bell but his life is a beautiful example of discouragement turned into victory. Lyte was an ordained minister. But he was, the story goes, a sad and burdened man as he neared the end of his ministry. He thought he had accomplished very little during his life and he was very disheartened, old, tired and infirm. The doctor told him he had only a few months to live. One evening — in a dejected mood — he started to thumb through his Bible and it fell open to one of his favorite passages.

As he read and re-read those familiar comforting words, all at once he was no longer old and tired. He no longer was sad and burdened, no longer discouraged. Words raced through his mind and he put them down on paper; and in less than an hour, he had written one of the most beautiful and inspiring hymns of all time: *"Abide with me; fast falls the eventide; the darkness deepens; Lord, with me abide; when other helpers fail, and comforts flee, help of the helpless, oh abide with me."*

Few people today know the name of Henry Francis Lyte, but the soul-stirring hymn he wrote in less than an hour, one hundred years ago, is known and loved all over the world. Yes, he was discouraged but from that point on, he made the best use of positive thinking and outlived his doctor.

THE FOURTH KEY — VISION

The fourth key is VISION — being able to picture the success we want to enjoy as public speakers. We have to know what we really want and we have to accept the fact that it will take effort to get what we want.

I remember reading about a very amazing Christian who lived in this country in the 1700s. Needless to say, he certainly knew the meaning of the word "effort" and what it took to accomplish his goals and to make his vision become a reality. His name was John Woolman and he was a person with a tremendous gift of faith and enthusiasm. More important, however, is the fact that he knew how to get *others* to make their own faith come alive so that it became a reality in their everyday lives.

Woolman was a Quaker and at that point in American history, many wealthy Quakers owned slaves. Woolman vowed that he would see to it that the Quaker people got rid of this blight of slave-holding and for 30 years he devoted himself to that task.

According to reports on his activities, he did not antagonize others or hold mass rallies. He didn't publish vindictive sermons against slavery or those who practiced it. Instead, he traveled the length of the land, visiting with slave-holders — asking them questions about how it felt as a child of God and as a Christian to own slaves.

There was no condemnation in his approach. He believed these slave-holders were responsible people with consciences and he would ask them: *"What does owning slaves do to you as a moral person?" "What kind of an institution are you passing on to your children?"*

You've probably guessed by now what his results were. Imagine! Years BEFORE the Civil War started, most Quakers had stopped the practice of owning slaves, thanks to the efforts of John Woolman. Quite an accomplishment, wasn't it? He had a vision and he held it until it became a reality.

What is *your* vision of a successful public speaker? If you will expend a fraction of John Woolman's effort (and it certainly won't take 30 years) you, too, can achieve an honorable personal goal.

THE FIFTH KEY — COMMITMENT

The fifth key is COMMITMENT to self. Too many people try their hand at public speaking *for only a limited time* without disciplining themselves to an on-going training program. Their fickleness reminds me of St. Augustine, who as a young man loved wine, women and song and occasionally he would pray: "Dear Lord, make me a good Christian, but not yet." That's the way I view a lot of non-committed persons— "Dear Lord, make me a good speaker, but not yet."

Do you remember the tale about the rich and wise man who gave his gardener the name of a special kind of tree he wanted him to plant? The gardener, however, protested, "That tree won't reach maturity for 200 years!" And the wise man replied, "In that case, there's no time to lose. Plant it right away."

THE SIXTH KEY — PROGRESS

The sixth key is to have a sense of *measured* PROGRESS. Rome wasn't built in a day. Or as Cavett Robert says, "You can't throw an egg out in the barnyard and expect it to crow tomorrow."

You need to program yourself to take small, definite steps toward becoming a better speaker.

- Mark your calendar right now and determine that you WILL sign up for a membership in a public speaking training group. Tell others about your commitment so you won't chicken out at the last minute (who wants to be embarrassed by trying to explain to your spouse or co-workers why you backed out?).

- Vow to read one book a week on public speaking (or one magazine article).

- Immediately start an outline for a brief talk that you would like to give. Start with an outline of yourself. You'll gain confidence discussing a subject you know extremely well, so that first outline should be ABOUT YOU.

- Read one self-esteem quotation daily. Better yet, prepare a series of cards that you can rotate on your bathroom mirror or dresser top or refrigerator or office desk.

- Subscribe to *Success Magazine* and *Guideposts Magazine.*

- Start a personal file of quotations which describe how you feel about life and its challenges.

- Pray for guidance and courage and if you haven't been to a house of worship recently, may I suggest that you return — on a regular basis?

THE SEVENTH KEY — ACTION

The seventh key is ACTION. If you still plan to drag your feet, just consider this poem by Robert Beck, which appeared in *The Kleinknecht Gems of Thought Encyclopedia:*

> The sands of Time that slowly flow
> From out my hour glass
> Will all too soon have ebbed away.
> My life will then be past.
>
> So I must make the most of time
> And drift not with the tide,
> For killing time's not murder,
> It's more like suicide!

Your ship will never come in if you don't send one out. I wish I could remember all the times I told myself I would start an exercise program, or start dieting, or do something else positive. I've stalled a lot of good programs and the reason is: I *REALLY* DIDN'T *WANT* TO DO THOSE GOOD, HEALTHY, POSITIVE THINGS.

And I maintain that *you* don't really want to be a good public speaker, either, if you don't start and start right now. What's stopping you? I'll tell you—**you** are stopping you. If you need time, you can find it (you probably don't miss too many meals, or your favorite TV programs).

If you need motivation—get it (re-read chapters 1 and 2).

If you need extra cash to invest in your speech education, ask your employer or banker for it.

If you need more resource material, get a library card.

BUT, JUST GET WITH IT!

Ladder of Success

100%	I did
90%	I will
80%	I can
70%	I think I can
60%	I might
50%	I think I might
40%	What is it?
30%	I wish I could
20%	I don't know how
10%	I can't
0%	I won't

Chapter 7

How And Where To Improve Your Public Speaking

"Life is now in session — are you present?"

Several years ago, as a young businessman, there was a period of time when I became very frustrated. I felt as if a dead-end had been reached within my company. I thought I had been put on "hold" and that I would wind up as "just another number" in a large corporation. I knew that I *had* to get someone's attention, that I needed visibililty in order to get back on track within the organization so that I might benefit from promotion opportunities.

I fussed and fumed about it for weeks on end. I also went

through a stage of reading all of the positive thinking material I could get my hands on. In fact, I read so much of it I wanted to gag. Slowly but surely, it dawned on me that all the reading in the world wouldn't do any good unless I got off my rear and *acted* in a decisive, positive way. I realized that opportunity might knock, but it wasn't going to turn the knob and walk in.

A friend of mine by the name of Jim Thomas had been encouraging me for months to join a local speech club. However, I always found some excuse to turn him down because I didn't have enough intestinal fortitude. But he never gave up pestering me about it. One morning he popped into my office and said, "Max, our speech club meets tonight and I'd certainly like to have you as my guest. How about it?" I replied, "Jim, I know it's a worthwhile organization but let me think about it and I'll call you before 5 o' clock and let you know." Jim turned and left, and I know he was thinking, "Same old story; same old brushoff."

I brooded about it the rest of the day and finally it hit me that THIS might be the way I was looking for to get that attention I craved within our company. Why? Because we never ever had any volunteers for the occasional public speaking assignments which came up.

So I called Jim, told him I'd go. That started me on an oral communications path that would later prove to be one of the wisest things I ever did.

THE TOAST OF THE TOWN

Jim's speech club actually was an official arm of the Toastmasters International organization, which was founded in 1924 by one Dr. Ralph C. Smedley. Dr. Smedley believed that the power to communicate is one of man's great endowments. Membership in each local club is limited to 40 persons and meetings are held weekly — some are breakfast clubs, some meet at lunchtime and still others gather at the dinner hour. There are about 100,000 members world-wide. It is a nonprofit organization.

Members help one another through a structured program of

speech-giving and attendant evaluation. The overall atmosphere is one of congeniality, helpfulness, education, personal growth. I learned to give short impromptu talks and later, longer speeches of a more formal nature. No speech is ever given, though, that does not receive the aforementioned evaluation. Evaluators help the speaker by pointing out areas where the speaker might improve, such as in the use of gestures, vocal variety, eye contact and speech composition.

After I had been a club member for about two years (and even gained enough courage to participate in some local speech contests), word got around my company that Max Isaacson would be a good candidate for any important presentations which might be forthcoming.

I WAS STUNNED

Soon after, I was called to the vice president's office. He said to me, "Max, we need someone to give a 30-minute report, complete with visual aids, to our company's board of directors concerning our new million-dollar computer system."

Even though I was eager to accept, I was somewhat stunned by the magnitude of the challenge. He wanted ME to speak to some two dozen directors of one of the nation's largest corporations, and on a subject on which I had only limited knowledge. Nevertheless, I accepted. Earlier I had *wanted* this kind of attention but little did I realize how it could materialize in such a big way.

Three weeks later, I made the presentation. It went nicely and I must have impressed them because I received a tremendous number of executive compliments and peer praise. It was a red-letter day for me, and it never would have happened without the valuable speech training from Toastmasters. A short time later I also was given a large increase in salary plus new responsibilities within the company.

In fact, this exposure to Toastmasters resulted in a number of business and personal gains in subsequent years. Through inter-state and inter-nation speech contest competition, I eventually was named to the Toastmasters International Hall of

Fame, one of the most exciting events in my life. I know speech training can help you, too, if you are faced with similar frustrations in your life.

IMPORTANCE OF COMMUNICATIONS

The Toastmaster organization asks its prospective members (men and women who are at least 18 years of age) to consider the following:

- Are you aware of the importance of communications to your success in business, industry, and the community?

- Can you present your viewpoint effectively on the spur of the moment?

- Do you speak articulately to others, individually or in groups?

- When you speak with supervisors or employees, do they understand your instructions and follow them through to satisfactory completion?

- Among your friends and business associates are you considered knowledgeable on current events?

- Are you ever asked to assume a position of leadership by your employer or by a community organization?

- If an assigned speaker or member of a panel in an organization to which you belong fails to appear, can you fill in on the program?

- Do you willingly accept assignments to present oral reports?

- Do you know how to serve as the chairman of a committee?

- Are you comfortable as a conference leader at business meetings?

In the event *you* don't have a Jim Thomas around to nag you, let me suggest some speech training options which you might explore.

First, most communities have some form of adult education and invariably, public speaking is one of the subjects offered.

Check with your local school board.

Larger cities have Dale Carnegie training programs.

Larger towns and cities also have one or more Toastmasters clubs, which I described above.

NATIONAL SPEAKERS ASSOCIATION

Then there's the National Speakers Association, which was founded in 1973 to provide a common platform for those interested in increasing the quality, integrity and visibility of the speaking professional, although nonprofessional speakers may join, too. The organization schedules workshops and an annual convention, publishes a newsletter and distributes cassette tapes.

The International Platform Association is similar in its objectives to the National Speakers Association. One of its early members was the renowned Lowell Thomas.

All of the above offer good, constructive programs. One with an *ongoing* program is very important, however, because no one will become an accomplished speaker unless he or she *continues* to use the training received. And most of us need regular attendance at such a club in order to *insure* that we receive continuing exposure. The example I always use to stress this point is: You wouldn't take just 10 or 12 piano lessons and then consider yourself an accomplished pianist. You definitely need to find a way to practice, practice, practice and the only way a public speaker can enjoy the right kind of practice is *before an audience.*

Let me emphasize here, however, that I'm not attempting to minimize the importance of *any* type of speech training, whether it be at public school adult education, colleges and universities, Dale Carnegie, or what have you. They're all good but just make sure you don't lose your momentum.

SEMINARS, BOOKS AND CASSETTES

Other profitable ways to gather speech tips include seminars, books and cassettes. Perhaps you even will want to consider forming a speech club within your own company or town. Let me add that a variety of ages — young adults, middle-agers and older adults — is advisable. Include both men and women, too. In other words, get as representative a cross-section as you can of society as a whole, because your "outside" speeches ordinarily will be given to a similar cross-section of the community.

I also would strongly recommend your joining the National Speakers Association or the International Platform Association if you want to eventually become a **professional** speaker.

The following addresses may be of help to you:

Toastmasters International
2200 North Grand Avenue, P.O. Box 10400
Santa Ana, California 92711

National Speakers Association
5201 North Seventh Street
Phoenix, Arizona 85014

International Platform Association
2564 Berkshire Road
Cleveland Heights, Ohio 44106

Dale Carnegie & Associates, Inc.
1475 Franklin Avenue
Garden City, New York 11530

Public Speaking Seminars
c/o Max D. Isaacson
2215 Ingersoll Avenue
Des Moines, Iowa 50312
(please include a stamped, self-addressed reply envelope on
personal requests for information)

Also check the yellow pages of your local telephone directory under the heading "Public Speaking Instruction."

LEADING AUTHORITY

Charles A. Garfield, Ph.D., is recognized as one of the world's leading authorities on improving human performance and productivity. He actually holds *two* Ph.D.s — one in mathematics and one in psychology. As a mathematician and computer analyst, he worked with NASA on the 1969 Apollo mission. As a psychologist and educator, he is currently on the clinical faculty of the University of California, San Francsico, School of Medicine.

Garfield has written more than 40 articles for professional journals, several books, including *Stress and Survival,* and is the author of the audio cassette program *Achieve Peak Performance,* published by the Nightingale-Conant Corporation.

He also is an outstanding athlete — he lifted weights at the 1964 U.S. Olympic trials and was a world-class power lifter. "But what," you may ask, "does all of this have to do with public speaking?" Please bear with me!

A few years after his Olympic trials experience, Garfield and some Russian colleagues conducted a very interesting experiment in peak performance. This experiment resulted in a rather remarkable result — it enabled Garfield to lift far heavier weights than he could have lifted otherwise. The method? MENTAL REHEARSAL!

As a result of this experiment, Garfield says he learned an important lesson: the lesson of how we all limit ourselves — sometimes severely.

He continues, "What I learned was an appreciation for the power of mental rehearsal. What the Soviets and many American researchers as well have learned is that if you can imprint deeply enough — if you can imprint those images in the mind's eye deeply enough — the brain and central nervous system, where all those memories are recorded, do not know the difference between a deeply imprinted image and the actual physical experience. We can, in fact, imprint many, many realities — many, many events, many, many actions in the mind's eye — and actually store those realities in the brain and central nervous system.

PUBLIC SPEAKING, TOO

"What all this means is that we can practice — without physically practicing — public speaking, athletics, relationship situations, artistic activity, business efforts and many other kinds of human endeavor. We can literally etch in the mind's eye and influence our capabilities for success by deeply imprinting success images — images of peak performance."

According to Garfield, *expectation* is an important element, that is, you must expect and believe that the positive outcome will occur. This positive belief, he says, serves to reinforce positive outcome. "It's esential that you put your will and energy behind the image," asserts Garfield. "We're not talking about idle daydreaming. We're talking about an effective and powerful way of influencing peak performance."

He continues, "There are many examples of peak performers who use mental rehearsal. Jack Nicklaus, the famous golfer, in his book, *Golf My Way,* says, 'I never take a shot, not even in practice, without imagining three things: my swing, the trajectory of the ball and where the ball lands. Not even in practice do I ever take a shot without first practicing mental rehearsal.'

EVEN JAIL NO HANDICAP

"The man who finished second to Van Cliburn, the great pianist, in the 1958 Tchaikovsky competition was one of the most revered musicians in the world. He was a pianist from the People's Republic of China. Shortly after the Tchaikovsky competition — a major one — he was thrown into jail, during the Cultural Revolution, and kept there for seven years. For seven years he could not go near a piano. Shortly after his release, he was back on tour and judged musically superior to the time that he was thrown into jail — musically superior after not having practiced for seven years.

"Many of the journalists who wrote stories about him asked the same question: 'How could you have improved? You haven't practiced in seven years.'

"What he said, of course, was 'I've done nothing but practice for seven years. *I practiced in my mind every single day.'*

"What he was saying was that in order to survive, he practiced the piano in his mind over and over and over — and actually improved his performance.

DEVELOPING YOUR POTENTIAL

"There are many other examples — many important examples — of mental rehearsal. We find them in daily life. We find them in many situations in which high performers are practicing their art form, their business or their sport.

"One of the things we're suggesting — which may be different from what you've heard before — is we're talking about not only improving skills you already have but also adding new ones — further developing your potential. Mental rehearsal, the master skill, is one of the key ingredients in this process."

Steven J. Granberg, a wellness consultant in Des Moines, recently shared with me some of the inner-person techniques which have been a tremendous help to him in his public speaking. He told me that not long ago he spoke to a class of 50 psychology students and during the presentation, everything seemed to go wrong. His slide projector jammed, his tape recorder malfunctioned and an associate failed to show up to assist him. Nevertheless, he lectured confidently for an hour and fifteen minutes, receiving a hearty round of applause when he finished.

DISASTER TURNS INTO APPLAUSE

"My self-confidence was the key to starting with an apparent disaster and ending with applause, " said Steve, adding, "My inner affirmations that I was a skillful speaker and that I would give an effective presentation helped me ease through a stressful situation to do what I had set out to do."

According to Steve, self-confidence to the speaker is like the keystone of a building. It is upon that which the rest of the structure is measured and dependent.

Steve went on to tell me that Henry Ford said, "Whether you think you can or whether you think you can't, you're right!"

He adds, "What we believe about ourselves determines what we will attempt, what we will persist in and what we will eventually accomplish. Stories ranging from *The Little Engine*

That Could to *The Man Who Would Be King* bring home the idea that belief in yourself shapes your confidence and accomplishments.

"Beliefs are easily understandable if thought of in terms of self-talk and self-perception. Self-talk is simply the words we use to describe ourselves and our situations. The person who believes the statements 'I am an effective speaker' and 'My speech will be well received' will speak with more confidence than will the person who believes 'My speaking abilities are questionable' and 'This crowd looks menacing.' "

YOU GET WHAT YOU EXPECT

And he says that while the reassurance and other emotional benefits of positive self-talk may be obvious, there are also skill-oriented benefits to the practice. As you identify yourself as an effective speaker, you spend more time in the practice of speaking. Moreover, as you believe in a receptive and supportive audience, you respond to the audience's positive feedback, moving in a mutually beneficial direction. Speakers, says Steve, like most people, tend to get what they expect.

He asserts that much of our self-talk was originally told to us by someone else: a parent, teacher, co-worker or friend. These statements by others can become part of our belief system, whether we actually remembered the statements or not.

We can improve our belief systems, he says, by consciously repeating positive statements to ourselves. "Self-perceptions, like self-talk, are learned associations," says Steve. "We have been taught them and we can re-learn them. Butterflies in the stomach, sweaty palms, shaky knees and stage fright have long been associated with public speaking. No wonder speaking is the most often stated anxiety, ahead of spiders and snakes! As we improve our self-talk and self-perceptions so we will increase our confidence and speaking abilities."

He recommends certain steps for improving self-talk and self-perception, including such affirmations as:

"I am developing my speaking abilities."
"I am an effective speaker."

"I am calm and in control when I speak."
"My speech will be well received."

BARBARA TROY'S STORY

Men and women from all walks of life are finding fulfillment through public speaking but many have learned that they must work very hard to be successful at it. Barbara Troy is one such person. Barbara is a professional speaker, seminar and workshop leader, owner of a training and marketing company, director of a pre-school center, member of the National Speakers Association, and president of her women's church organization in her home town of Booneville, Missouri. She is married and the mother of four children. She is positive, energetic, enthusiastic and motivating. A recent seminar participant said, "Barbara doesn't need a computer — she is one!"

But it wasn't always that way. Barbara is just one of thousands who have worked diligently to become effective public speakers even though they had certain handicaps in their formative years.

"Labeled as a child too stupid to spell and always the last one picked for kick ball, my self image was painted in all negative shades," she told me. In later life, after a series of uneventful jobs, she decided to have some vocational testing done. The results weren't impressive.

"After being told that I shouldn't do anything that in any way concerned the medical field, due to a weak stomach, they decided that I was not 'ideally suited' for anything!" she says with a sense of humor. "Then, I heard a speaker say 'when you find something you really love to do, so much that you would do it for recreation, then you have found your profession.' I set out to find mine. Surely, I must have talent. Everyone else did.

"By age 30, I had never read a fiction book (a condition I don't recommend) because I wanted to build a 'natural resource file' within myself. Through my cassette player, Dottie Walters, Paul Meyer, W. Clement Stone, Thomas Winninger and countless others revealed their secrets of success. Attending classes, workshops and seminars, I found that others took notes on the contents of the presentation and I made notes on the speaker's delivery, what equipment he or she used and how the speaker dressed. As luck would have it (luck being defined as working hard enough, often enough to be in the right place at the right time), I was asked to speak to a convention of several hundred sales people.

"THEY TURNED ME ON"

"Somehow, when they turned on the microphone they turned me on, too. It was fantastic! I had found the 'love' the speaker told me about. Now to find out how to market it."

She subsequently sent "freebie" letters to church and civic organizations to have a testing ground for her material. This eventually opened doors for her paid engagements. Moreover, in order to give herself more time to be with her growing family, she found others to do the things she didn't like to do, such as mending, cleaning bathrooms, washing windows and so on.

"My theory on mending was to keep it in a cute basket until the kids outgrew it and then to secretly dispose of it. Unfortunately, I couldn't get my husband to outgrow anything. Although my kids didn't care who cleaned the bathroom or for that matter if it was cleaned at all, they did care who held them, read to them or went for walks in the woods with them. You can't eliminate all the things you don't like from your life, although it would be nice. To eliminate as many things as you can will really improve your attitude."

After more "free" talks than she would care to recall, she began to charge a fee for her speeches. "When I suggested hanging a 'Rent Me' sign on my body, a friend declared I'd probably charge too much. When one client said, 'is that all you charge for what you do?' I doubled the fee and got it."

Her particular seminars are on time and personal resource management, organization, verbal communications, family team building and total effectiveness for women. What about self-confidence during speech delivery?

"I am plagued with ever-present fears," confesses Barbara.

"Will I be good? Will this presentation meet the needs of the audience? Will I be able to get the audience working with me? Learning to take the energy from the fear and to direct it into my presentation was the answer. I've heard it said, 'if ye are prepared ye shall not fear.' Preparation is hard work that always pays off. Who is the audience and what are their needs? Total research of the material is necessary and you must always keep it up to date. The meeting room, equipment and even my introduction are all prepared before the presentation.

PREPARE TO SERVE

"There is no way I can control everything; I can only prepare. The only thing within my control is my own attitude. My most important job is to prepare my mind and prepare to serve my audience. Then I can place myself in the position of Ethel Merman, who said, 'I know my lines; what is there to be nervous about?' "

Here are her points for the beginning speaker:

- Spend the time necessary to decide what you want. Break it down into progressive steps and begin to work toward it.

- Associate with others who share your interests and goals. Give, listen and learn.

- Develop a relationship with your cassette recorder. Spend your time with tapes of the people you admire and respect in the speaking profession.

- Listen more than you talk.

- Make time for what is important to you. Plan your recreation (re-charging) time.

- Remember the only thing you can control is your own attitude.

- Research your material until you are an expert.

- Join a professional speakers association, get involved and work hard.

Listen to the exhortation of the dawn!
Look to this day, for it is life —
The very life of life!
In its brief course lie all the verities
And realities of your existence;
The bliss of growth,
The glory of action,
The splendor of beauty;
For yesterday is but a dream,
And tomorrow is only a vision;
But today well-lived
Makes every yesterday a dream of happiness,
And every tomorrow a vision of hope.
Look well, therefore, to this day!
Such is the salutation of the dawn.

From the Sanscrit

"Three things matter in a speech: Who says it, how he says it, and what he says. Of the three, the last matters the least."

LORD MORELY

"To talk much and arrive nowhere is the same as climbing a tree to catch a fish."

CHINESE PROVERB

Chapter 8

How to Prepare
A Speech

"I don't dance, but I'd love to hold you while you do."

We've all heard the expression that "success in life is a journey, not a destination." Success in public speaking likewise is a journey, a journey that should begin with a little "road map" to show us the destination we want to reach.

That road map is WHO, WHAT, WHEN WHERE, WHY and HOW.

WHO is the audience? Are they adults, children, teenagers, business persons, farmers, engineers?

WHAT is their purpose in asking ME to speak? Is it a special occasion? Is it because I have knowledge of a certain subject that thay want to hear about? Am I strictly entertainment for them or am I to share important information? Is this to be an "after dinner" speech? Will there be other speakers on the program?

WHEN are they convening? In a week, two weeks, a month, or six months from now? Morning, noon or night?

WHERE are they meeting? In a convention hall, a restaurant facility, a company conference room, a church? In this city or someplace else?

WHY are they assembling as an entity? What is their purpose for being (i.e., Lions Club, political caucus, community fund drive, sales training)? Will it be a formal, semi-formal or casual meeting?

HOW long do they want me to talk? Can I apply what I know and what I do to make their meeting a rousing success?

Dr. Robert H. Schuller has a definition of success that I sincerely believe we should apply to every single one of our public speaking efforts, and it is this: *"Success is building self-esteem in yourself and others through sincere service."*

If you can't increase your self-esteem, if you can't give sincere service then I think you should seriously consider declining an offer to speak. For example, I will not speak to a group that has scheduled a late dinner preceded by a "long" social hour with cocktails. Their minds will be too numb for me to hold their attention and as a result I will be unable to maintain my self-esteem or theirs.

AS YOU PREPARE YOUR SPEECH

But let's assume you **can** fulfill these criteria by accepting. The Who, What, When, Where, Why and How questions will enable you to ANALYZE YOUR AUDIENCE, which is essential if you are to assemble the proper material for your speech.

In Chapter 9 I'll show you how I structured a speech based on the analysis of my audience — a high school graduating class. Obviously, the serious part of my message and the humorous part of my message had to be suited TO THAT PARTICULAR AUDIENCE.

That brings us to my second point — USE APPRO-PRIATE MATERIAL. Considerations concerning the use of appropriate material include age, educational level, sex, experience in the area of your primary subject, whether the audience is **expecting** to be entertained in addition to being informed on a topic, *and what the program chairperson has suggested to you.* I can't stress that last point about the chairperson too strongly — especially if you become a **paid** professional speaker. You'll find that one of your primary objectives as a professional speaker is *to make the chairperson look like a hero!* You not only owe the chairperson the best effort you are capable of but he or she also is your ticket for later referrals. The chairperson knows what previous speakers have used effectively (or ineffectively) and additionally may have established an overall theme for the meeting or conference.

As you'll learn in the next chapter on humor, most experienced speakers do recommend the use of a least some humorous material, regardless of your primary subject. But in any event, NEVER USE ANY BLUE MATERIAL. Down-in-the-gutter type jokes aren't appropriate for any public speaking situation that I can think of. Why be crude when the English language has so much to offer?

THE JOKE BOMBED

I'll never forget the time I was at a business seminar which was attended by about 98% men and 2% women. The seminar leader made a few welcoming remarks and then he decided he wanted to tell "a story." He added, "This probably isn't very appropriate for the women in the audience so I wonder if they would excuse themselves and come back in about five minutes?"

The women left, all right, and they never came back. The seminar leader went on with his smutty story and didn't even get a laugh from the men. I don't know when I've seen a more inept speaker. So skip the blue material — most men don't care for it, either. Of course, some listeners can be offended by **anything** and it's doubtful that you can satisfy all the people all the time but if in doubt about the nature of your humor or other material, leave it out.

When delivering your speech, make your GESTURES natural and unaffected. You don't have to stab the air or pound the lectern or otherwise be theatrical (unless that's the way you **always** communicate). If you can arrange it, have your presentation video taped and study the playback to see if you can learn from it.

VALUE OF GESTURES

Suzy Sutton, who is a professional speaker and trainer, firmly believes in the value of natural, genuine gestures. She writes:

> A flick of wrist
> A twinkling eye
> A threatening fist
> A poignant sigh
> Gestures all
> however slight
> Are stabs at darkness
> and rays of light

She believes that gesturing effectively is a skill and that awareness is the first step to improvement.

"We can," she says, "project a personality that's pleasant and appropriate if we take the time to analyze, understand and improve our body's vocabulary of movement."

Similarly, while I encourage VOCAL VARIETY, that is, to refrain from a boring monotone, emphasis can be easily made by a slight raising of the voice or a lowering to almost a whisper. Avoid being too mechanical but again, don't be too affected, either. Record every speech you make on an audio cassette recorder and analyze it later.

NOTES OKAY

What about the use of NOTES? If you're more comfortable

with notes, use them! There is a Chinese proverb to the effect that the weakest ink is more enduring than the strongest memory. In formal speech contest competition, it's almost considered a weakness to use notes. But who says you've got to be a macho speaker? Heck, I even know a Protestant minister who *always is careful to keep a TYPED copy of the Lord's prayer with him at the pulpit in the event he might forget part of it.* It's no sin to use notes. Just don't make them a big crutch. It's perfectly okay to glance at them during your speech, particularly if that's going to make you more relaxed. Some of the best speeches I've ever heard were given by speakers who used notes.

I think the *form* of your notes is relatively important, however. Try to know your material well enough to condense your notes to a 3x5 or 4x6 card. There's no point in distracting your audience by flipping large sheets of paper or having a fistful of cards. The odds really are in your favor that you won't need extensive notes, but if you do need a security blanket, let me suggest a compromise: KEEP A 3x5 CARD AT THE LECTERN TO GLANCE AT AND MORE DETAILED NOTES OFF TO ONE SIDE. That way, if you really need them or draw a total blank, merely reach for them to bail yourself out.

REHEARSE TEN TIMES

I must admit that one fear most of us have is totally forgetting what we want to say next. A few seconds seem like an eternity when you blank out. It's okay to pause while you're trying to remember something and it might help if you merely repeat the last point you were making.

But conscientiously *rehearsing* your speech about 10 times or so will make a big difference in your retention of material. However, if you feel you *must* read most of your speech, then . .

- Memorize the opening
- Memorize most of your main points
- Memorize the close, and make it a really moving conclusion

Some speakers like to read their speech but they have learned to outline it in a manner that permits lots of eye contact with the audience and it also "prompts" them on vocal variety and gestures. I use an outline I call it a "Reader Prompter." Here's an example:

READER PROMPTER

The speaker can see a complete subject line,
LOUDLY   feeling confident in front of the audience
without worrying about lost ideas or words.
        Underlining the key thoughts in the speech
helps to maximize eye contact and the complete
GESTURE   speech can be spaced in such a way
that VISUAL STOPS occur throughout.
These stops let the speaker
insert vocal and physical movement prompters
QUIETLY   to enhance the presentation.
As a result, the speaker's delivery is
        less formal in appearance
SLOWLY   and listeners will not
                know how much is being read
                and how much is ad-libbed.

Earl Nightingale has published a great deal of material on public speaking and he offers the following tips on speech preparation:

- Perhaps a good rule to remember is to write the speech out completely whenever it is likely that someone will want a copy of it . . . or whenever it is important that we not deviate from the text.

- I still write my speech out completely, word for word, whenever I have a particularly important speech to make. Then I run off a copy or two on the copier so that I can mark up the original. I then proceed to go over the speech again, carefully, with a felt tip pen, making additions, deletions, underscoring, drawing little stars, putting in numbers and generally rendering it incomprehensible to anyone but me.

EXTRA COPIES

- I take the copies of my speech with me in my briefcase in

the event the program director, or company head, or whomever wants a copy for reproduction and distribution to those in attendance.

- There is material that lends itself to memorization . . . such as great quotations, bits of poetry, great ideas that we may want to include in several of our talks and so on. But the main thrust of our speeches, in order to remain fresh and up-to-the-minute, must constantly change.

- One of the reasons a person who does not speak often seldom makes a really interesting speech is because he never does any preparation work until he knows he has a speech coming up. The regular speaker is looking **all** of the time. He hunts for items of interest the way a Minnie ball collector walks over an old battlefield; he misses very little.

BE A GOOD READER

- The person who does a lot of speaking will usually have a fine library, be a good reader, and have a good working knowledge of his language.

- If you're writing a speech and you're not sure of your grammar, especially syntax, have a person who is more knowledgeable on the language edit it for you.

- If you are at all unsure of a word's pronunciation . . . by all means, look it up and check it carefully.

- Mispronounced words drop like bombs into an audience.

After considerable research on my part, a fair amount of speaking experience, lots of discussion and just plain listening, I believe that I have isolated those elements of good speech which can spell success for you.

1. Make your speech title ARRESTING! Create an aura of mystery. Stimulate interest. So many speeches have bland titles. I'm sure many would-be listeners think "Ho, hum." You've heard some of these bland titles, like . . . "How to Succeed" or "10 Keys to Wisdom" or "More Effective Management" and so on. I believe titles are like your suit of clothes. People will judge you before you ever open your mouth, so make your title a good one.

Put a little pizzazz in it. Study some of the titles in book stores to get an idea of what attracts attention and prompts interest in the product.

Awhile back I used the title, "IF I CAN'T TAKE IT WITH ME, I'M NOT GOING!" It was a real play on words and when the emcee read it, it created laughter before I even got to the lectern. The point I subsequently developed had to do with my being "my brother's keeper" and that we had to take love with us always.

On another occasion, I went with, "I DON'T DANCE, BUT I'D LOVE TO HOLD YOU WHILE YOU DO." I then proceeded to discuss the value of romance in our lives and how my wife and I first met.

A friend used the title "ARE YOU A SUCCESSFUL FAILURE?" His main thrust was to cite examples of seemingly successful and wealthy people who wound up committing suicide, becoming drug addicts and so on. But he had our attention from the outset because of what appears to be a contradiction.

"BEAUTIFY A JUNKYARD—THROW SOMETHING PRETTY AWAY TODAY" is a title I used for a speech which suggested that all of us should use better and more loving language in our communications wasteland.

2. Start your speech with an ATTENTION-GRABBING OPENING so your listeners will sit up and take notice immediately. For example, I began a speech on mental health with this: "SUPPORT MENTAL HEALTH OR I'LL KILL YOU" Another started with: TELL ME, IS THERE LIFE AFTER BIRTH?"

In a talk to a group of businessmen, I started with this: "*A beggar approached a well-dressed man on the street, stopped him and said, 'Mister, do you have a dollar for a cup of coffee?' 'Of course not,' replied the well-dressed man, adding, 'If you are that bad off, I should think you would be humble enough to ask for a dime or a quarter instead of a dollar.' The irritated beggar fired back, 'Mister, give me a dollar or give me a dime, but please don't tell me how to run my business.' "*

That led to my discussing the impact of government controls on our respective businesses.

Considerable listener interest was garnered when I began another speech this way: *"I recently read that the preamble to the Declaration of Independence contains 300 words, the Ten Commandments has 297, the Gettysburg address comes in at 267 while the Lord's Prayer has fewer than 100 words. However, a recent report from the federal government on the pricing of cabbages has 26,911 words. I will confine my speech to something between the Lord's Prayer and the pricing of cabbages."*

The reference to word length built interest and by the time I got to cabbages, the audience was in a state of great expectancy.

3. Utilize a VISUAL AID of some kind because the audience retention of your subject is *six times greater than without*. In the opening mentioned above, I held up a large head of cabbage. I never worried about losing the audience from that point on.

I gave another speech that opened with a negative statement about my direct-mail industry, a quote actually lifted from a major newspaper. I knew the statement was misleading so as soon as I finished reading it, I shouted *"That's a bunch of baloney"* and I simultaneously slammed down a ring of the real baloney meat. Again, the audience was with me all the way from the opening to the end. A little corny? Perhaps, but our objective in public speaking is **to be successful communicators,** isn't it?

Naturally, more sophisticated visual aids can be used to assist you in your presentation and these might include color slides, three-dimensional exhibits or simply a flip chart. If you do use a chart, for goodness sake make sure the printing is large enough to be seen from the last row of the audience. How many times have you seen people strain to see what the presenter had on his or her chart? A good many times, I'm sure.

4. Relate PERSONAL EXPERIENCES as tie-ins with your speech subject. Your listeners definitely will have a deeper interest in what you are saying when they know you have actually experienced what you are talking about. No one is going to pay much attention to an armchair quarterback. The person who has been in the arena is the person who's going to be heard. The members of the audience don't want to hear theory, they want eye-witness accounts.

Many persons have approached me to say that they have difficulty coming up with subject matter for a speech. I usually answer as follows: If you want to give a good speech, you need self-confidence. If you want self-confidence, you need to know the subject matter. If you want to know the subject matter extremely well, talk about something that you personally have experienced. Need some of my personal examples? Okay, here they are!

- I received severe facial burns from a stove when I was about five years old and this gave me material for a speech on safety in the home.

- Because my own parents lacked much formal schooling, I learned to deeply appreciate the value of higher education, and I have driven this point home in talks to high school students.

- A hassle I once had with a church committee prompted me to analyze my own motives and resulted in a speech on the importance of love and understanding.

- I frequently write letters to the editor of our local newspaper and these are fuel for speeches on current events.

- Seeing a high school girl with just one hand perform brilliantly in a basketball tournament provided me with speech material on courage and perseverance.

- The death of a co-worker's little girl prompted still another talk on the need for child-like faith in our Creator (she had left a very sensitive, moving diary to her parents in which she had asked them not to worry about her, adding that she was not afraid to meet God).

- Someone I know very well is an alcoholic so it's not difficult for me to gather speech material on drug addiction and its impact on society.

- Another fellow employee opened his home to his elderly *mother-in-law* and did it in a very loving way — a way that impressed me so very much that I subsequently worked it into a theme for a speech.

When you talk about those things you have experienced, you lend credibility and sincerity to the talk. You also automatically have confidence in your subject matter because **you** are the one who has experienced it.

We all have strengths, loving experiences, foibles and skeletons in our closets but we can be open about it and share these with our listeners. At the same time, we needn't sound "holier than thou."

EVERYONE LOVES A STORY

I don't know how to explain it, but people do indeed love to hear stories. *There's something about a tale that creates deep interest and maybe that's why Jesus talked in parables when explaining things or making points with his disciples.*

Leo Rosten says no more powerful words of communication have been invented by the human race than these four: *"Once upon a time."* And there is a promise, he says, in those four words that five will surely glorify the end: *". . . they lived happily ever after."*

Sometime ago I gave a laity day sermon in my church and I wanted to make a point about love. The usual treatment of the subject seems to require that the speaker (or the preacher) quote St. Paul's statement on "faith, hope and love."

Instead — I told a story. A true story. A story about a very loving individual by the name of Lee Shapiro.

I had met Lee, who is an attorney, last summer at a speakers' convention. He's sincere, warm, enthusiastic, loving. There's nothing phony about him. One of the things he likes to do at various gatherings is to greet people with a big bear hug and then he plants a little adhesive-backed red heart on their lapel. Obviously, he knows how to make friends fast and most of the people at the convention were wearing his red hearts.

DOES SOCIAL WORK

I learned that he likes to do social work back in his home state of California and will spend many hours visiting various institutions, such as those for the aged and the handicapped. It seems that he recently visited a facility for the mentally retarded and was going through the wards giving his bear hugs and hearts to staff and to patients, accompanied by the head nurse and her assistant.

It was lunchtime, and as he passed one room, he looked in and saw a young man in his 20s who was eating lunch. The young man's name was Leonard, and he had food smeared all over his mouth, his face and his chest, and at first Lee thought, "Maybe I'll pass him by for now and return some other time." But then he changed his mind, went in and gave the young man an enthusiastic hug and planted a red heart on him.

The young man, Leonard, started to grin from ear to ear, and made some gutteral noises as if he were trying to say something. And as Lee Shapiro turned to leave, he noticed that the head nurse and her assistant were wiping tears from their eyes. "I'm sorry," said Lee. "did I do something wrong?" And the head nurse replied, "Not at all, Mr. Shapiro. You see, until just now, Leonard hasn't smiled or tried to talk for more than 10 years."

Isn't that a *beautiful* story? And it's not preachy. It's contemporary and graphic. I've used that illustration of love several times since that sermon and by the time I finish with it, I swear that you could hear a pin drop. That's why I always encourage speakers to use stories to illustrate their points. And if you can tug at the heart strings, so much the better.

USE PERSONAL EXAMPLES

Even when talking about *someone else's poignant experience, tie it some way to you personally.* For example, you could say, *"One day at lunch, a day when I was feeling a little blue, I chanced to read about a man who really knew how to chase the blues away. How did he do it? He did it by losing*

himself in service to others. I'd like to share it with you . . ."
Then proceed to tell the story.

A lot of speakers find it difficult to work a story into their speech. They just yank it in abruptly and it loses syntax and fluidity. I've worked at this especially hard and I don't believe you could mention any story on any human subject or any human event that I couldn't subtly and believably work into my speech. After all, almost everything that happens **is** human drama and you can relate it *some* way to your subject, whether it's motivation, time management, sales or what have you.

Let me give you another example. Let's say you have to give a speech to a trade association. That association, by its very nature, is *service* oriented or it wouldn't be in existence. Moreover, every business or governmental entity I can think of provides some kind of service. And good service is generated from personal desire to help, and that spark must come from within oneself. The Lee Shapiro story certainly is an excellent example of self-motivation. It's a good story to use.

The Lee Shapiro story also could be used to enhance a presentation on . . .
   . Giving to the United Way (giving one's
      time as well as money)
   . Self-sacrifice
   . Motivation
   . Enthusiasm
   . Thoughtfulness
   . Service to the handicapped
   . Mental retardation
   . Love

5. Use VOCAL VARIETY, which I mentioned previously. When asked for the three most important elements of his art, the Greek orator Demosthenes replied, *"Delivery, delivery, delivery."* Speed up your delivery occasionally (minds will drift when the speaker is using a slow rate of speaking); slow down for emphasis; drive home a point by raising your voice; lower your voice or use pauses to dramatize another point.

Quite often you'll find during a speech that two people in the audience will be whispering to one another and this can be distracting to the speaker as well as to the audience. The fastest way to stop their rudeness is for **you** to stop your speech. It doesn't take much of a pause on your part before you have everyone's undivided attention again.

I've heard a lot of good speakers over the years who had beautiful-sounding voices but they became almost too mechanical in their delivery. Zig zag once in awhile. Use a little animation. Move away from the lectern (if you have a hand-held mike).

6. Try to use HUMOR, especially if the joke is on you. Please see Chapter 9 for a full treatment of the subject of humor.

7. BE ENTHUSIASTIC, even if it doesn't come naturally. On most other personal points, I believe a speaker should be as *natural* as possible and without airs of affectation. But I make an exception when it comes to enthusiasm because I believe enthusiasm is contagious and an audience needs to be caught up in your enthusiasm.

I know a guy who frequently speaks in public. At times his grammar is atrocious, his subject isn't always the greatest and he dresses so wildly that his attire really detracts. However, he consistently is one of the most enthusiastic speakers I know. You can't help but jump on his bandwagon because he puts such great energy into it. And before you know it, you've overlooked all his other faults and find yourself thinking, "GO, MAN, GO!"

I know it's tough to always *feel* enthusiastic and I guess I would tell you to at least *try* to always *look* enthusiastic. If you do, a great deal of the time you actually will *become* enthusiastic in the process.

The plodding, lacklustre speaker will lose an audience in a hurry. And although the speaker might indeed feel deeply about the subject, it takes an outward display of fire to arouse the audience to the same level of intense feeling.

Other than being enthusiastic, I don't believe we should

role-play or try to be something or somebody we aren't. BE YOURSELF! There have been many times when I thought I should try to copy someone but I never felt comfortable and actually felt phony trying to act the part of another.

8. BE PLEASANT and smile as much as possible during your delivery. Most subjects aren't that grim. Some years ago, *Quote Magazine* said, "While great progress has been made over the last 50 years in communications devices, there is still a lot to be said for a smile." And a Chinese proverb says, "He who cannot smile ought not to keep a shop."

9. Always have a GOOD APPEARANCE. This means apparel as well as posture. Don't let your clothes speak louder than you and if you are a woman, don't wear gaudy, jangly jewelry. You want people to concentrate on your message, not on your ornaments.

10. BE BRIEF, generally speaking. Unless you have been engaged by a program chairperson to speak for a whole morning or afternoon, be brief. Please pardon the sexist reference but a macho friend says, *"A speech should be like a woman's skirt: long enough to cover the subject but short enough to be interesting."*

11. Keep uppermost in your mind that YOUR AUDIENCE WANTS YOU TO SUCCEED, so step to the lectern with the thought that you have friends "out there," not enemies.

12. Record every speech you give and give it an honest self-appraisal. Also have someone else critique it for you. Analyze it to see what you could improve the next time. Do it *especially* if you have bombed. There have been many times when I gave a speech that didn't seem to go over with the audience and I really had to force myself to play the tape back. In other words, I was very reluctant to re-live a painful presentation but by doing so, I was able to check things like vocal variety, the humor which got laughs and the humor that didn't, continuity, and so on.

13. PRACTICE, PRACTICE, PRACTICE! Use a mirror and your tape recorder. Make a dry run in front of your speech club. Some people advocate rehearsing in front of one's spouse. I don't because your spouse or some other close friend isn't likely to be objective in your case. Moreover, most speech material — if it's going to make an impact — needs a larger number of listeners. How can you tell if a joke is good or not if you tell it to a single listener? You can't, because the success of a great deal of humor depends on a ripple effect of a good sized audience. I'll tell you this, I'd much rather speak to 500 than 5 any day.

14. Use PLAIN TALK, particularly if you are presenting technical information to lay audiences. Too much of the time a speaker will think he or she has to embellish a talk with big words instead of using conversational-level words. Just because you are talking in public doesn't mean you have to change your manner of word usage. Keep it simple.

Here's an example of what I'm talking about — a utility executive communicated to customers this way:

> *The realization that fossil fuel resources are finite has mandated that wasteful utilization of these fuels be eliminated. Consequently, efforts to determine the efficiencies of alternative energy uses are finally receiving deserved priority . . . . The abundance of electric fuels, however, is not sufficient reason to warrant their indiscriminate use in a conservation-oriented political environment.*

What he was trying to say was simply this: Fuel is limited and shouldn't be wasted.

One of my pastors used another good example sometime ago in his sermon: Jesus said to his disciples, "When you are preaching, who do you say I am?" And one of the disciples answered, "Lord, we tell the people that you are *the eschatological manifestation of the ground of our being, the kerygma in the humanizing process.*" And Jesus responded, "Whaaaaaat?"

If the speaker uses words which are not clear to the listener, he or she might as well speak in a foreign tongue.

GOOD ENGLISH IMPORTANT

Using plain talk doesn't mean that you should be careless about observing the rules of good English. Earl Nightingale tells us, "Every grammatical mistake stands out like a giraffe in a herd of field mice. It stops everything, it makes educated people stop listening to what's being said and wonder why the person made such an obvious mistake. People who believe sloppy or poor English is all right as long as you're one of the 'good old boys' are wrong. It may be all right telling stories around the card table, but the trouble is you form bad habits which have a way of popping up when you wish they wouldn't."

Nightingale says one of the legendary Vince Lombardi's cardinal rules of excellent performance in life and football was continuous review and practice of *the fundamentals*. Setting a goal and remaining everlastingly at its accomplishment in life is the key.

"And it's the same with becoming and remaining a fine public speaker," asserts Nightingale. "Once the basics are understood and applied, then it's a matter of practice, practice, practice."

15. Talk about PEOPLE, not things. And personalize it and localize it if you can. Talk about people you work with, play with, love with, worship with, cry with, dream with.

One time I wanted to dramatize the uncertainty of this life we live and the fact none of us knows whether we'll live to be 9 or 90. I could have given medical data on longevity, I could have said that the average age in this country is increasing, that philosophers have long addressed that issue, that many of us live in fear of living and fear of death, that we pop zillions of pills into our mouths each year to obtain some stability in our stressed lives.

But rather than talk about statistics, I elected to talk about the 9-year-old daughter of one of my co-workers, whom I mentioned earlier in this chapter. The little girl suffered from Reyes syndrome and she knew that her prospects for living were very bleak. She lapsed into a coma, which lasted about two weeks. She died.

A few days after the funeral, the father and I were discussing his family's adjustment to the tragedy and he told me a remarkable thing about his deceased daughter. He said they found a diary that she had kept right up to the time that she went into a coma, and she left this mesage: *Dear Mom and Dad. I know I have a serious illness but I don't want you to worry. I think I have led a good life. I'm not afraid to die and I'm not afraid to meet God."*

That true story was, in my opinion, a poignant, personalized, localized way to make a point.

16. Have a memorable close. Give the audience something to take away with them. I frequently close with a poem or a memorable quotation and many times I've been approached after a speech by someone who wanted a copy of it. Now and then, I'll even preprint copies of the poem or quotation and offer free copies at the end of the speech. If you're in business, print your company name at the bottom and this can be a good form of advertising.

Let's review again the 16 points I've just made. They are:

1. Make your speech title ARRESTING.
2. Start with an ATTENTION-GRABBING OPENING.
3. Utilize a VISUAL AID if possible.
4. Relate PERSONAL EXPERIENCES as tie-ins.
5. Use VOCAL VARIETY.
6. Try to use HUMOR.
7. BE ENTHUSIASTIC.
8. BE PLEASANT.
9. Always have a GOOD APPEARANCE.
10. BE BRIEF.
11. Remember that YOUR AUDIENCE WANTS YOU TO SUCCEED.
12. RECORD every speech for critiquing.
13. PRACTICE, PRACTICE, PRACTICE.
14. Use PLAIN TALK.
15. Talk about PEOPLE.
16. Have a MEMORABLE CLOSE.

If you do all of the above, I'm sure you will give an exceptional speech. The next question we need to ask, however, is: What are the actual components of a speech structure? My good friend and speech mentor — Sam Zickefoose — set an excellent example for a good many speakers in my state and I always thoroughly enjoyed hearing him talk.

He gave me much valuable assistance several years ago when I participated in an international speech contest competition. I distinctly remember sitting in his living room, discussing the finer points of speaking. Sam had been a successful competitor before me in the same kind of competition. Some of his wisdom I've saved for the last chapter in this book, but Sam firmly believed that if a speaker would follow a definite outline when preparing a speech, success was virtually guaranteed. Here's what he suggested:

FORMULA FOR SPEECH OUTLINE

I. **Opening** (attention getter)
     A. Unusual statement or fact.
     B. Dramatic effect.
     C. Surprise.
     D. Create curiosity.

II. **Bridge** (to lead into theme)
     A. Situation story.
     B. Humorous story (must fit).
     C. Develop reason for theme.
     D. Compliment listeners.

III. **Body** (limit 3 or 4 points)
     A. * Illustrate with a story
     B. ** Illustrate with a story.
     C. *** Illustrate with a story.
     D. **** Illustrate with a story.
          (if a longer speech)

IV. **Summary** (review main points)
     A. Re-style for variety.
     B. Count for emphasis.
     C. Build up for close.
     D. Be brief.

V. Closing (same dramatic power as 1)
   A. Dramatic statement.
   B. Poem.
   C. Moving story.
   D. Relate to subject.
   E. Stop suddenly.

Note: Numbers 1 and 5 should be memorized and have some dramatic value.
*From weakest to strongest.

Use this for *your* next speech and I'm confident you'll be a winner, too. But always remember your *real* success can be measured by the self-esteem you build in yourself *and* others THROUGH SINCERE SERVICE.

SPEECH CONSIDERATIONS

1. Date_____ Location _____ Time of Day_____
2. Audience   a) Number in attendance? _____
                b) Men and women? _____
                c) What kind of club or organization?_____
                c) What is background of average person? _____

                e) Are there any members of audience who can be pulled into speech some way?

                f) Is audience young, old, or middle aged?_____
                g) Will audience have been drinking before hand?_____
                h) Are there any ethnic considerations? _____
3. What theme does the organization want the speaker to develop? What are the topics of presentors who will be preceding me or coming after me? _____
4. What problems (or other experiences) has the audience had recently?_____
5. Is the date of this speech during a special season, holiday, or event?_____

6. What has been the audience's experience with the speaker's particular business or industry? Can the speaker poke fun at himself or herself as a result? _____

7. Speech development:
       a) Main theme _____
       b) Title _____
       c) Opening _____

       d) Main body _____

       e) Conclusion _____

       f) Thought-provoking close _____

Other get-ready things:
       a) Chairman's introduction of you (write it out and hand it to him).
       b) Lectern, microphone and other facilities adequate?
       c) Has hostess been instructed that there is to be absolutely no removal of dishes (or coffee pouring) after program has started?
       d) Any hand-outs planned?
       e) Fee to be charged? When will it be paid?
       f) Name, phone number of co-ordinating chairperson: _____

       g) Background information on the organization you are going to address: _____

       h) Has the organization received any awards for excellence or are there any other complimentary things you can work in the speech? _____

REMEMBER: Eloquence comes from the heart. Make them glad they they asked you to be their speaker!

CHAPTER 9

What About Humor?

"He who laughs, lasts."

"Who was that lady I saw you with last night?"
"That was no lady — that was my brother. We've had trouble with him lately."

One of the many things public speakers agonize over is whether to use humor in their presentations. And if they do use it, what kind and how much? Victor Borge tells us, "Laughter is the shortest distance between two people." I would add that it's also the shortest distance between a speaker and the speaker's audience.

Most experienced public speakers in almost every situation believe in the prudent use of some humor — from the president of the United States on down. Humor disarms, it relaxes, it entertains. And if it is self-deprecating, it cuts the speaker down to size and shows that he or she, too, is just a common person who puts on pants one leg at a time.

SHORT AND FUNNY

Humor also can make an effective point. For example: "You can't go wrong if you follow the Mickey Rooney approach to public speaking: Be short and funny."

Bob Orben, long known as the master of the one-liner, is one of the most talented comedy writers around. Author of some 45 books of professional-level humor material, he has written for a number of TV stars and has been a speechwriter for leading business and political figures, including President Ford.

He also publishes a semi-monthly comedy newsletter. A typical sampling includes: "I'm sorry I'm late. I followed an oil company executive at Confession. Had to wait four hours and fifteen minutes."

"My wife has recently become interested in science. She's trying to figure some way to run jumper cables from Burt Reynolds to me."

PUTTING DOWN PEOPLE

Bob believes "the magic of humor is that it indicates a certain trust. If two people can laugh together, it indicates a certain acceptance of what the humorist is saying — it's a building of trust." And humor is being perceived more and more as a healing agent, he says. "Humor can soothe, heal, build — and destroy." Much of the present-day humor, according to Bob, concentrates on putting down people and institutions. "It's easy to write this kind of humor," he says. "it's the other kind — the humor that singes without burning — that's hard."

He continues, "Psychiatrists will tell you that one of the first signs of mental illness is the loss of a sense of humor. And the first sign of recovery is the ability to see a humorous aspect, even in a sea of troubles, and smile at it. I have found the common trait among well-adjusted people with handicaps — blindness, loss of hearing, or other physical infirmities — is that they have a pot of jokes about what is the matter with them."

What does he advise those of us who would like to use humor? "Plan ahead. You can develop a body of humor to use in given situations if you give it some thought. Most of us have a body of humor that's based on situations or questions frequently asked of us. For example, my wife and I don't have any kids. I can't tell you how many times we're asked, 'Do you have children?' My reply is always, 'No, I had a very strict mother-in-law.' . . . . So it's a good idea to develop a body of material that will cope with any given situation."

PRESIDENT'S STORY

President Ronald Reagan used to tell the joke about a businessman who ordered a floral arrangement for the grand opening of a new branch office. When he got there, he was shocked to find that the wreath that was delivered bore the inscription, *"Rest in Peace."* The businessman became angry and on the way home he stopped in at the flower shop to complain. But the florist interrupted him and said, "Wait a minute. Just look at it this way: Somewhere in the land today, a man was buried under a wreath that said, *'Good luck in your new location.'* "

In my opinion, there's no one funnier than Erma Bombeck and she has tried to put her finger on the secret of creating humorous material. She writes, "There are two things that should never be researched. One of them is what makes people laugh. The other is the love-making habits of consenting adults. In some cases, it's the same thing."

She continues, "No one has been able to pinpoint what makes people laugh because people are reluctant to talk about it. Polls and seminars have been tried, but people say if you think about it too much and talk about it too much, you lose the spontaneity, the mystery, the joy that made it so special in the first place. It holds no surprises for anyone."

LAUGHTER IS THE BEST MEDICINE

Almost everyone is aware of Norman Cousins' phenomenal recovery from a near-fatal illness. Cousins says he was "greatly elated by the discovery that there is a physiologic basis for the ancient theory that laughter is good medicine."

In his book *Anatomy of an Illness as Perceived by the Patient*, Cousins relates how he did everything possible to laugh (viewing funny movies, reading joke books, listening to nurses tell humorous stories, and so on) and how the positive chemical changes in his body ostensibly helped in his healing.

He also tells how a great humanitarian felt about humor. "Albert Schweitzer always believed that the best medicine for any illness he might have was the knowledge that he had a job to do, plus a good sense of humor. He once said that disease tended to leave him rather rapidly because it found so little hospitality inside his body . . . . Albert Schweitzer employed humor as a form of equatorial therapy, a way of reducing the temperatures and the humidity and the tensions. His use of humor, in fact, was so artistic that one had the feeling he almost regarded it as a musical instrument."

He shares another story about Dr. Schweitzer. " 'Some of my steadiest customers are referred to me by witch doctors,' Dr. Schweitzer said with only the slightest trace of a smile. 'Don't expect me to be too critical of them.'

THE SECRET

"When I asked Dr. Schweitzer how he accounted for the fact that anyone could possibly expect to become well after having been treated by a witch doctor, he said that I was asking him to divulge a secret that doctors have carried around inside them ever since Hippocrates.

" 'But I'll tell you anyway,' he said, his face still illuminated by that half-smile. 'The witch doctor succeeds for the same reason all the rest of us succeed. Each patient carries his own doctor inside him. They come to us now knowing that truth. We are at our best when we give the doctor who resides within each patient a chance to go to work. The placebo is the doctor who resides within.' "

The preceding may appear to be pretty heavy stuff in a chapter devoted to the use of humor, but I wanted you to see some relationships which may help you in your own use of humor, particularly in public speaking.

Incidentally, Mr. Cousins shares the following humorous story in his book.

> There was a priest who was playing golf and he had difficulty in hitting the ball over a small pond. After he put five balls in the water, he hesitated before teeing up again, then said to his caddy: *"I know what I'm doing wrong. I just forgot to pray before each shot, that was all."* He prayed, then swung at the ball—and it traveled about twenty yards in a loop right into the water. *"Father,"* asked the caddy, *"might I make a suggestion?" "Certainly, son"* the priest said. *"Well, father,"* the caddy said, *"the next time you pray, keep your head down."*

WHAT WILL WORK?

What the heck is funny material, anyway? What makes a good joke? How can you tell **ahead** of time what will work with an audience and what won't? If someone had guaranteed answers to those questions, he or she could make a million a year writing for all of the TV and nightclub comedians in the country. There are, though, some things which can be learned about this subject which will help you in your quest for ways to apply humor in your speeches.

Dr. Laurence J. Peter and Bill Dana, in their book *The Laughter Prescription,* tell us, "A vital sense of humor is based on an ability to cut loose from our customary mode of thinking. It is the ability to be playful with that which customarily is thought to be serious. A fully functioning sense of humor must be iconoclastic, impulsive, irreverent and impertinent. We must delight in being uninhibited. Take any conventional conduct and visualize the most unconventional or contradictory behavior and you have the essence of humor. Take the most accepted thought and then give it the most unconventional treatment and you have created humor .... Incongruity is central to all humor. Something that does not fit the generally accepted mold — something out of context, unexpected, illogical, exaggerated, unreasonable or inappropriate — seems to be the essential element of humor."

In a book which has become a Bible for humor craftsmen, *Enjoyment of Laughter*, author Max Eastman lists four laws of humor:

- The first law of humor is that things can be funny only when we are **in fun**. There may be a serious thought or motive lurking underneath our humor. We may be only "half in fun" and still funny. But when we are not in fun at all, when we are "in dead earnest," humor is the thing that is dead.

- The second law is that when we are in fun, a peculiar shift of values takes place. Pleasant things are still pleasant, but disagreeable things, so long as they are not disagreeable enough to "spoil the fun," tend to acquire a pleasant emotional flavor and provoke a laugh.

- The third law is that "being in fun" is a condition most natural to childhood, and that children at play reveal the humorous laugh in its simplest and most omnivorous form. To the child, every untoward, unprepared for, unmanageable, inauspicious, ugly, disgusting, puzzling, startling, deceiving, shaking, blinding, jolting, deafening, banging, bumping, or otherwise shocking and disturbing thing, unless it be calamitous enough to force them out of the mood of play, is enjoyable as funny.

- The fourth law is that grown-up people retain in varying degrees this aptitude for being in fun, and thus enjoying unpleasant things as funny. But those not richly endowed with humor manage to feel a very comic feeling only when within, or behind, or beyond, or suggested by, the playfully unpleasant thing, there is a pleasant one. Only then do they laugh uproariously like playing children. And they call this complicated thing or combination of things at which they laugh, a joke.

He concedes, though, that all attempts to explain humor have failed. Moreover, he says a joke is not a thing, but a process. "And the process, although it comes so natural to playful minds, is not simple. I can analyze any joke you bring me, if you will leave it overnight — for the task requires reflection — and give you in the morning the chemical formula upon which it is composed. And it will always be composed of unpleasant experiences playfully enjoyed, combining in various orders, degrees and proportions with pleasant experiences. That is all that a joke is or can be."

He emphasizes the importance of arousing emotional interest in your listeners, to "be interesting."

He also lists "the ten commandments of the comic arts," which are:

1. **Be interesting** (you must arouse an emotional interest on the part of your listeners).

2. **Be unimpassioned** (while you must arouse feelings, you must not arouse feelings that are too strong and deep).

3. **Be effortless** (don't use dragged in jokes or say "that reminds me of ").

4. **Remember the difference between cracking practical jokes and conveying ludicrous impressions** (practical jokes have to start off *plausibly* and collapse *suddenly*. A ludicrous impression can be preposterous right from the start).

5. **Be plausible** (the speaker must take the audience with him wherever he *purports* to be going; let the listener participate vicariously).

6. **Be sudden** (a joke has to be kept up the sleeve and then "sprung" or "cracked" suddenly. Don't give the point away in advance of the ending).

7. **Be neat** (a "neat" joke is one which requires no stretching, or patching, or inferential bridgework; it is not lame, forced or far-fetched).

8. **Be right with your timing** (jokes have to be sprung, they have to come as a pleasantly unpleasant surprise to a mind that is on the way to something else).

9. **Give good measure of serious satisfaction** (it helps if your humor can make a point).

10. **Redeem all serious disappointments** (calculate the degree and kind of satisfaction necessary to redeem a violated feeling, and turn a shocking flippancy into a jovial and immortal joke).

In this same book by Eastman, he mentions others' definitions of humor. For example, Art Young said "Why we laugh is generally because we have seen or heard something that is at variance with custom."

James Thurber said, "Humor is a kind of emotional chaos told about calmly and quietly in retrospect... Human dignity, the humorist believes, is not only silly but a little sad."

Gelett Burgess was quoted as saying, "The first source of comedy is found in the well-known theory of Frustrated Expectation... Our minds have associated ideas connected by thought-tracks much like the network of a railroad system. Procedure along these tracks gives ideas that are logical, or at least natural or normal. In the comic, however, there is a frustration of the logical process, much as if a train jumped the track, arriving at an unexpected terminus."

Most of us do not intend to be stand-up comics or even deliverers of snappy one-liners, but most of us would like to thread a humorous **story** or two through our speech material.

Dr. Charles Jarvis, a Texas dentist and certainly one of the top humorous speakers in the country, is an expert at this. He also compares a successful humorous story to the train track analogy. He says a funny and unexpected punch line can be compared to a train "jumping" its tracks — there is a surprise ending to the trip.

For example, here are some typical Jarvis witticisms:

"Man comes into my dentist office, Says, 'Doc, what kin I do for yellow teeth?' I tell him, 'Wear a brown tie.' "

"Another time a guy comes into my office and says, 'Doc, do I have to floss **all** my teeth.' And I replied, 'No, only the ones you want to keep.' "

"People today want something for nothing. A wife says to her husband, 'You have to do something for our son.' He says, 'Do something for him? I bought that business for him. I showed him how to keep books, records, inventories, stayed with him six months.' She says, 'I know, but he and I were talking, and he's going bankrupt.' 'I know he is, honey, but what else can I do?' 'Well, he's wondering if you will buy him out.' "

Jarvis said during 12 years of dental practice, he soon found out that he had to use humor because the most frustrating thing in a dentist's life is to be the only one who cares. "People like their hubcaps better than their teeth."

HUMOR, A MEANS TO AN END

Jarvis' speeches involve about 85 percent humor and 15 percent message. But he never tells a story that doesn't relate to the subject.

Several months ago I attended one of his humor seminars in Dallas and he spent the better part of a day discussing humor, its essence, the nuances in using it, and why it often succeeds and sometimes fails. Like Max Eastman, Jarvis maintains that an audience must be "in fun." He told of his experience addressing a large audience — a trade association — which had just completed a bitterly-contested election of officers. Obviously, that audience was not "in fun" and Jarvis recommends, to the extent possible, that you try to get a group like that **back** "in fun" if your humor is going to be appreciated.

I asked him to share with me his thoughts on handling fear. He told me, "Fear — I have had lots of it. Walking home late at night as a boy 11 years old, after helping change the marquee at our local Brady, Texas theater. Going through the hazing program at Texas A. & M. Then, of course, the flying off a carrier — at night! Being catapulted off the deck of a small carrier, into the night with no horizon, just as though you were thrown into a closet — now, that's a thrill. Then the kamikaze attacks during the war, plus the two typhoons where we rolled so much the carrier deck dipped water, when we were supposed to capsize at 41 degrees. All of this I stood through the use of one of our greatest gifts — courage and mainly a **sense of humor**. The latter I tell my audiences is a gift from the Creator to handle the problems one cannot solve."

Cavett Robert, mentioned in earlier chapters and a friend of Dr. Jarvis, says that in order to make a speech, you have got to have a good, dynamic message **riding on the wings of humor**. In order to get the audience to remember it, you have to have stories throughout that illustrate the point.

Gene Perret has an interesting book out called *How to Write & Sell Humor*. Gene has been a comedy writer for Carol Burnett, Bob Hope, Phyllis Diller, Bill Cosby, and others. What does he say about humor? "There is only one ultimate judge of comedy and that is the audience. The rest of us are merely guessing. Some of the pros are better guessers than others, but even the best cross their fingers and hope the audience will respond."

IN THE MIND OF THE LISTENER

Gene says that in using humor, you must remember that a good joke is not in words, gestures or anything you do from the platform. Rather, he asserts, the joke is in the mind of each member of the audience. "You can tell a fantastic story and get great laughs," he adds, "yet someone in the audience may nudge a neighbor and say , 'I didn't get it.' Why? Because for some reason the picture didn't form in that person's mind. Consequently, to that person, it isn't a joke."

Podium Humor is the title of a very entertaining book by James C. Humes. He writes, "The German philosopher Immanuel Kant has said, 'The essence of humor is an expectation that comes to nothing.' It is the collapse of a developed pattern. In other words, the punch line deflates the build-up. The poor guy gets his hopes up and then **pfttt**."

He continues, "Aristotle once explained humor as 'the pleasurable distortion of what is expected' — the familiar in an unfamiliar place."

He shares the following humorous story:

A minister friend of mine was asked to speak at the Rotary Club on marital sex, but when he was asked by his wife about his speech that night, he just mumbled the first thing that came into his head — yachting. Afterward, on the street, a neighbor came up to his wife and said how much they all liked the speech. "Really," she said. "I'm somewhat surprised. There are only three times he tried it. Once he got sick and the other times his hat blew off."

BREVITY IS THE SOUL OF WIT

In his book *How To Be A Successful Emcee*, LeRoy Stahl suggests, "Find out what is funny about your audience, your speaker, or his subject. Make your own contribution to posterity by devising a humorous approach to one of these subjects, keeping in mind all the while that brevity is the soul of wit. Deliver your comments with a consistently cheerful countenance and you will get a reasonable number of laughs.

"Pausing for laughs without seeming to do so is one of the most important things that you have to do when trying to get them. Unless you give your audience time to laugh, its members will 'dry up' on you because each person will keep quiet in trying to hear what you have to say next. Pause while the audience laughs. Then start again before the laughter dies entirely away.

"Also to keep the audience laughing, you should give some reaction to your own allegedly funny remark, an arrested gesture or a facial expression; although if you are working alone as a speaker or monologist, such a reaction must be very slight . . . . It is your reaction, tiny though it may be, that really gets the laugh. It confirms your audience in the viewpoint that what they heard was intended to be funny. Therefore they feel much safer in giving way to the release of laughter."

You may not remember what Erma Bombeck told us in an earlier chapter: "One of the hardest parts of delivering a humorous speech is the patience to wait out the audience. Don't panic and let them come to you. It takes an uncommon amount of guts."

ON GOD'S SIDE

I don't know who said it but I like the observation that "God loves humor — that's why he made monkeys and men."

Many of you have overcome tremendous handicaps — be they physical, mental, emotional or social. But please keep in mind that nothing is more useful than the ability to laugh at our own defects while we are trying to improve them. Lincoln made fun of his homeliness. During a debate Douglas accused Lincoln of being two-faced. Without hesitation Lincoln replied: "I leave that to my audience. If I had two faces, would I be wearing this one?"

You may be wondering how, specifically, you might go about obtaining humorous material for a certain audience. At the end of this chapter I have listed some resource material which you may find helpful. But let me give you a detailed approach from out of my own experience.

I was invited to speak to a high school graduating class sometime ago and I wondered how I could say **anything** meaningful to those youngsters who were young enough to be my own children. How could I relate to them? How could I introduce a little humor to pave the way for a sincere message that I wanted to impart? I wanted to keep the overall presentation light but still, I wanted to get across an important point about the value of **ongoing** education and helping humanity.

Using the "SPEECH CONSIDERATIONS" sheet which I showed you back in chapter 8, I finally produced the talk which follows. It was very successful and not too "preachy," which I knew would turn the kids off anyway.

Note that I . . .

• Prepared my own introduction and gave it, in easy-to-read typed form, to the Master of Ceremonies. This introduction gave my necessary speaking "credentials," told that I was the father of teenagers, and finally warmed the audience up by putting me down with the "hot air" remark.

- In my opening, I made myself sound overly pompous by stating that "I can hardly wait to hear what I have to say."

- I next singled out the graduating class' faculty adviser and put him in his place, so to speak, with "he's told me that many times." The kids laughed boisterously at this.

- At the time I gave the speech, we were in the midst of the energy crisis and the public was down on oil companies, so the youngsters easily could relate to the "obscene gestures" problem I had.

- I proceeded to localize the humor by talking about **my own family's** breakfast habits and dress habits. I did this later on with the driving problem with my son and compared him to a 5,000-mile check.

- I took a story I had heard earlier about airlines and adapted it to local high schools. Again, the youngsters roared when they heard that a competing high school couldn't tell time.

- Women's lib was gaining momentum so I injected a little humor about that. It's good to have **timely** topics as well as the old standbys.

- I next eased into the more serious nature of my talk by complimenting them. I also paid a sincere compliment to **their teachers.**

- Finally, I closed with the point I wanted to make all along, namely that there is great value in ongoing education and that brotherhood and caring about others ultimately is the real test and real education in life.

INTRODUCTION OF SPEAKER

Our guest speaker today is MAX ISAACSON, the administrative vice president of a local oil company. He attended Des Moines public schools and Drake University, where he obtained a B.A. degree in 1954. Last year, he was named to the speakers' "Hall of Fame" of Toastmasters International, in recognition of his contribution to that organization's worldwide program of better listening, better thinking, and better speaking. In the forty-year history of Toastmasters, only a handful of other Iowans have received similar recognition.

MR. ISAACSON is the father of three teen-agers and he confesses that his greatest accomplishment in life occurred just recently, when he managed to get the keys to the family car away from these teen-agers on a night when they ALL wanted to drive it.

This past year, he has addressed many audiences and because he has had to get **up** so often, he says he is living proof of the old adage that "hot air always rises." Please welcome our rising speaker, MAX ISAACSON.

East High Senior Class Breakfast Speech

Thank you for that fine introduction. It was so great that I can hardly wait to hear what I have to say. As a Des Moines native, I know of your school's fine reputation and I am aware that your vice principal, Don Powell, is very intelligent, an excellent administrator and a very humble person — he's told me that many times.

This is a special time for you and your asking me to be here is a nice gesture, and I'm not used to receiving nice gestures because I'm in the oil business, and a lot of people don't like oil companies anymore, and whenever I drive a company staff car, other motorists quite often give me **obscene** gestures. Since the energy crisis, I've seen enough upturned middle fingers to last me a lifetime, so I've learned to look out when driving.

As I look out on this sea of faces, I'm impressed with your extraordinary appearance. I'm not used to seeing people dressed like this for breakfast. My own kids usually show up in jockey shorts or cross-your-heart bras, looking like the end of a hard winter.

But all of you do look like the breath of spring and you have treated me very kindly here today. Earlier this morning, I asked one of the seniors what time it was and he very politely said: "It's 7:00 sir." If I asked what time it was over at Tech High, one of the ROTC cadets would have said: "It's zero seven-hundred hours," because that's the way they talk in the military. But if I asked what time it was over at Lincoln, **where they are a little slow to catch on,** the student would have studied his watch for a whole minute, and then he'd say: "Gee, I'm not sure what time it is, but the little hand's on the seven and the big hand's on the 12." That's the way the kids tell it at Lincoln.

Two of my four kids attend Lincoln right now and I'm living proof that insanity is hereditary, because I get it from my kids. I recently read that by the time the average person dies, he has spent two years of his life in the bathroom, three years in the car, and five years eating. That describes my son perfectly, and he won't even be 18 for another month. And you should see his bedroom — it's a real disaster area. He has wall-to-wall Pepsi bottles, Ho-Ho wrappers, dirty clothing, and a giant poster that says: "*Girls, conserve energy — share your body heat.*"

I'm telling you, my son is an accident looking for a place to happen. He spends so much time in our family car *that his rear end has to be checked every 5,000 miles.* His friends are really something, too. His friends have tee-peed our yard so many times, that we haven't had to buy toilet paper for over a year. It's saved us a lot of money.

Speaking of money, I've got a teen-age daughter who is money mad. All she can think of is money, money, money. I said: "Susie, money won't buy you friends." And she replied: "I know, dad, but it gets you a nicer class of enemies!" That's a woman's logic for you.

However, I believe that for women as well as for men, there is greater opportunity today than ever before. The women's lib movement has helped, too, and equality of the sexes has created such a stir, that I've noticed that the "help wanted" ads in the newspaper's classified section have to be worded very,

very carefully these days. There was an ad that actually appeared in the *Des Moines Register* not long ago that read: *"Wanted: Model for maternity clothes. Will accept either pregnant man or woman."* Another ad said: *"Go-go dancer wanted; must have good legs and no hair on chest."* That seems reasonable for this generation.

You people belong to one of the sharpest generations ever born. You are alert, attentive, clever, eager, keen, lively, sensitive, spirited, and quick to reason. And I believe that along with that, you have enough common sense to realize that, as someone has said, success in life is a journey and not a destination. I believe that firmly, and I believe in the value of ongoing education. At middle-age, I've just started to work on a Master's degree at Drake University, and I hope that **you** don't stop reaching for education in your journey, education that will enable you to be more of a positive influence on your fellow man. And being a positive influence certainly is one of the great things about the teaching profession. Someone has said: *"Teaching is a noble profession because teachers affect eternity; they can never tell where their influence stops"*. . . . Think about that for a moment: *"Teachers affect eternity!"*

Let me ask you a question. How will you affect eternity? Where will your influence stop? I would be crazy to try to convince you that a diploma in your hand is a ticket to a better life. It is not what you hold in your hand, but what you hold in your head and in your heart that will decide your destiny. I hope you'll carry in your head and your heart those moving words of Edwin Markham, who earlier in this century wrote: "There is a destiny that makes us brothers, none goes his way alone; all that we send into the lives of others, comes back into our own; I care not what his temples or his creeds, one thing holds firm and fast; that into his fateful heap of days and deeds, the soul of man is cast."

Ladies and gentlemen, I wish you the best of

destinies, and may God richly bless you!

LEARNING TO BE FUNNY

As I mentioned in Chapter 8, so often I'm asked: "Where do you get your ideas for speeches and for the humor you use in them?" I usually tell the questioner that the source of material is truly *all around us*. I get ideas from TV programs, from the personal experiences of co-workers, from business seminars, from newspapers and magazines, from my family, from just about everyone and everyplace — INCLUDING RESTROOM WALLS.

I once built a speech around graffiti I saw in a restroom. Someone had written, "I LOVE YOU!" Later, someone else had come along and had penciled in below it: "THANKS, I NEEDED THAT!" So how did I use that for a speech? Well, first of all it let me introduce a little humor in the speech itself because of the source of the information, i.e., the restroom walls. Then I developed the rest of the talk on how we so often fail to tell important people in our lives that we indeed **do** love them. Let me ask you, the reader, right now: How long has it been since you told even a member of your immediate family that you love them?

Another time, I was watching the Mike Douglas TV show and he had asked some 6-year-old youngsters to complete some of the real old cliche's. Answers were extremely amusing, like: *"A bird in the hand . . . might poo poo."* Another youngster said, *"People who live in glass houses . . . should keep all their clothes on."*

Wife/husband humor usually is well received and it certainly is something all of us married folks can relate to.

I told one audience. "My wife and I will celebrate our 25th wedding anniversary in June. It has been proved that married life is healthy and statistics show that single people die sooner than married folks. However, a guy I know who's been married four times says '**You may live longer if you're married but it's a s-l-o-w death.**' "

WE DON'T SLEEP FOR WEEKS

On another occasion, I said, *"My wife and I have a good relationship. The other day she asked me if I would love her when she's old and gray, and I said 'Of course — haven't I loved you through five other hair colors?' She wants to have her hair dyed back to its original hair color only she can't remember what it was."*

On still another occasion I said, "You've heard the expression 'Never go to bed mad at one another.' Sometimes my wife and I don't sleep for weeks."

Most husbands and wives take such humor good-naturedly, probably because there's a lot of truth to some of it. For example, the institution of marriage is undergoing changes. Religion writer Bruce Larson tells about the change in relationship between husband and wife after they have been married for a few years. He illustrates this by relating the seven stages of the common cold in the life of a young married couple.

> *The first year, the husband says, "SUGAR, I'M WORRIED ABOUT MY LITTLE SWEETIE PIE. YOU'VE GOT A BAD SNIFFLE AND I WANT TO PUT YOU IN THE HOSPITAL FOR A COMPLETE CHECKUP."*
> *The second year, the husband says: "LISTEN, HONEY, I DON'T LIKE THE SOUND OF THAT COUGH. I'VE CALLED THE DOCTOR AND HE'S GOING TO RUSH RIGHT OVER."*
> *The third year, it goes like this: "MAYBE YOU'D BETTER LIE DOWN, HONEY. NOTHING LIKE A LITTLE REST IF YOU'RE FEELING BAD. I'LL EVEN BRING YOU SOMETHING TO EAT."*
> *The fourth year: "LOOK, DEAR, BE SENSIBLE; AFTER YOU'VE FED THE KIDS AND WASHED THE DISHES, YOU'D BETTER HIT THE SACK."*
> *Fifth year: "WHY DON'T YOU TAKE A COUPLE OF ASPIRIN?"*
> *Sixth year: "IF YOU'D JUST GARGLE OR SOMETHING INSTEAD OF SITTING*

AROUND BARKING LIKE A SEAL, IT MIGHT HELP."
    Seventh year: "FOR HEAVEN'S SAKE, STOP SNEEZING! WHAT ARE YOU TRYING TO DO, GIVE ME PNEUMONIA?"*

You know something? That sounds just like my household.

Another one of our nation's top humorous speakers is **Roy Hatten.** Here's what he has to say on the subject:

"I cannot tell you how to be funny, but I can tell you why you are NOT. Because people who are NOT funny and don't use humor and can't use humor say, 'I can't tell a joke.' 'I can't remember the punch lines.' You have programmed yourself for failure right there.

"One of the things I try to stress in the use of humor is don't take yourself too seriously because everbody else quits when you do.

"You don't need to use dirty humor. There is twice the abundance of clean humor available. I use religious illustrations with humor. You have to develop judgment as to the kind of humor you are going to use. You cannot monitor your humor to the point where you are going to please everybody. I think some people come to hear a speaker just to be offended.

"Johnny Carson makes $81,000 a week for the Tonight Show. The President of the University of Michigan makes $65,000 **a year.** This tells me two things: The American people will pay a lot more money to be entertained then they will ever pay to be informed. Or public broadcasting would be the Number 1 network, right? And Laverne and Shirley would not be the Number 1 show, but it is. And you get paid for being funny and properly using humor. You may have the greatest message in the world but nobody wants to hear it if you don't make them feel good. **And that's basically what humor does — it**

makes you feel good within yourself. If you don't believe that you're funny then don't try, because you will not fool the audience.

"And you have to change your attitude before you attempt it.

"Here's my favorite story:
    "My brother-in-law is a 57-year-old effeminite bachelor. He has a pink belt in karate, and that may give you an idea. It's pink with just a little lace — nothing vulgar. And he has this English bulldog named Cecil — you know, with a flat face from chasing parked cars. He was down in New Orleans in the French Quarter one day. He brought Cecil along with him. The bar-tender says, *'All right, fella, what'll you have?'* in a sharp tone of voice. My brother-in-law says, *'Oh, mercy. I believe I'll have a little ol' scotch and water.'*

"And the bartender says, *'Look, we don't want sissy boys in this bar. There's a bar down the street for you fellas. Get out of here!' 'Listen, I'll have my bulldog attack you.'* Again, the bartender said, *'Look fella, we don't want you or the dog. Now get out of here.' 'All right, Cecil, sick him.'* Cecil the bulldog pounced over the bar, pinned the bartender against the wall and said, *'Bousy wow wow.'*

"You can use humor with inspirational material and in an illustration I use quite often, is an answer to your problem. In inspirational material I very often will quote scripture. I'm a Christian and I make no apology for that. Jesus is Lord of my life. You make your own choice — I made mine. I'm not your judge — you are.

FAITH CAN MOVE MOUNTAINS

"Do you realize Jesus could have finished his ministry in a year and a half if he hadn't had to explain things to Peter? Yah. The Bible is a credit card to the universe. In the first chapter you find the key to it — the phrase **'God said'** appears eleven times. He said it and it was. You do the same thing. You do it all the time.

" *'Well, I believe I'm catching cold.'* That's right! You just said it and you got it. I found out what programs your mind and whether you're funny or can tell humor properly is what you have said prior to this day about it. And if you want to use humor don't ever say *'I can't tell a story.' 'I forget the punch lines.' 'I just don't feel funny.'* You can change all that by changing your mind.

"The key to it is that you have two sets of ears. You've got an external set that you are using right now and you've got an internal set where YOU hear YOUR voice inside your head. That's what programs your subconscious. Example: *'Well, I can remember faces but I can't remember names.'* Everybody has said that all their life. What's the result? Anybody ever forget a face? No. But you don't remember the name because you told your subconscious you couldn't.

"I had a neighbor once who went outside in five inches of snow — barefooted — to get his newspaper. I yelled at him, *'You're going to die!'* He replied, *'No, I don't even catch cold.'* And he didn't!

"Then I began to realize something that Jesus was trying to explain to Peter one day. He said, *'The things that defile a man are not the things that go IN his mouth but the things that come OUT of it.'* Who is the only animal on the face of the earth that can select words? A human being.

"One day they were walking down the road and saw a fig tree. Jesus said a strange thing. Write this down: Mark 11:23. It's your license to be greater than you ever dreamed you are. Right out of the mouth of the Master — He said, *'Have faith in God.'* That's what it says in the King James version. In the Greek it says have the God kind of faith. What is that? What is the God kind of faith? It's believing in something you can't see. The Bible says if you believe it, then you'll see it. Natural man says, *'Well, I ain't gonna believe it till I see it.'* That's what Thomas said. It doesn't work that way.

"Jesus said to Peter, *'For verily I say unto you that whosoever shall say unto this mountain "Be thou removed, and be thou cast into the sea, and shall not doubt in his heart, but shall believe those things which he saith shall come to pass; he shall have whatsoever he saith." ' "*

"Four times he used the word *'say.'* One time he used the word *'believe.'* Absence of doubt.

"The thing I'm telling you is that if you don't believe that you are funny, neither will your audience and they can sense it. You've got to believe in the gift of the brain and the body that God gave you because it works. But you've got to understand how it works and that's why I recommend the Bible.

"Out of every 10 statements that man makes, seven of them are negative. Naturally negative. You have to learn to be positive. I love the Old Testament and the beauty of it. Psalms 141:3 is a great clue for you. *'Set a watch, O God, before my mouth.'* First of all, that we will give something of value to people when we dare to stand before them."

Yes, he who laughs, lasts. Or, as Johnny Carson has said, "Laughter is the common denominator of our lives. The more we learn to laugh with each other, the more we'll learn to live with each other."

And Fred Allen, one of this nation's all-time funny men and a radio legend, stated, "Maybe if we can find a common bond of humor to stop the fussin', fightin' and feudin' in the world, we might actually laugh our way into peace. In the final analysis, laughter is the universal language of mankind and a little nonsense now and then is relished by the wisest men."

"Humor is an affirmation of dignity, a declaration of man's superiority to all that befalls him."

R. GARY

"Comedy is an escape, not from truth but from despair."

CHRISTOPHER FRY

"We face our crises today with tears and dejection or with grins and determination. I prefer the latter . . . . As far as I am concerned, humor is not a luxury; it is a necessity."

FRANK MILLER — Pulitzer Prize-Winning Cartoonist

". . . he never knew a man who possessed the gift of hearty laughter to be burdened by constipation, I can readily agree with him."

NORMAN COUSINS

"What I want to do is make people laugh so they'll see things seriously."

WILLIAM R. ZINNSER

HUMOR RESOURCE MATERIAL
(Courtesy of Dr. Charles Jarvis)

Booklist

THE TOASTMASTER HANDBOOK; Herbert V. Prochnow; Prentice-Hall, Inc.; Englewood Cliffs, NJ

THE COMPLETE TOASTMASTER; Herbert V. Prochnow; Prentice-Hall, Inc.; Englewood Cliffs, NJ

THE SUCCESSFUL SPEAKER'S HANDBOOK; Herbert V. Prochnow; Prentice-Hall, Inc.; Englewood Cliffs, NJ

THE PUBLIC SPEAKER'S TREASURE CHEST; Herbert V. Prochnow; Prentice-Hall, Inc.; Englewood Cliffs, NJ

THE NEW GUIDE FOR TOASTMASTERS AND SPEAKERS; Prentice-Hall, Inc.; Englewood Cliffs, NJ

BRAUDE'S TREASURY OF WIT AND HUMOR;

Prentice-Hall, Inc.; Englewood Cliffs, NJ
SPEAKER'S ENCYCLOPEDIA OF STORIES, QUOTA-
TIONS, AND ANECDOTES; Prentice-Hall, Inc.; Engle-
wood Cliffs, NJ
BRAUDE'S SECOND ENCYCLOPEDIA OF STORIES,
QUOTATIONS, AND ANECDOTES; Prentice-Hall, Inc.;
Englewood Cliffs, NJ
SPEAKER'S ENCYCLOPEDIA OF HUMOR; Prentice-
Hall, Inc.; Englewood Cliffs, NJ
LIFETIME SPEAKER'S ENCYCLOPEDIA; Prentice-
Hall, Inc.; Englewood Cliffs, NJ
SPEAKER'S DESK BOOK OF QUIPS, QUOTES, AND
ANECDOTES; Prentice-Hall, Inc.; Englewood Cliffs, NJ
COMPLETE SPEAKER'S AND TOASTMASTER'S
LIBRARY (8 volumes); Prentice-Hall, Inc.; Englewood Cliffs,
NJ
THE LAUGHTER PRESCRIPTION; Dr. Laurence J.
Peter and Bill Dana; Ballantine Books, New York, NY
HOW TO WRITE AND SELL HUMOR; Gene Perret;
Writer's Digest Books, Cincinnati, Ohio
THE SPEAKERS HANDBOOK OF HUMOR: Maxwell
Droke; Harper and Bros.; New York, NY
CAVETT; Dick Cavett and Christopher Porterfield; Ban-
tam Books; New York, NY
THE FUNNY MEN; Steve Allen; Simon and Schuster;
New York, NY
BENNET CERF'S BUMPER CROP - Volumes 1 and 2;
Garden City Books; Garden City, NY
ESAR'S COMIC DICTIONARY; Evan Esar; Horizon
Press; New York, NY
FUN FARE; Reader's Digest Association; Pleasantville,
NY
THE JOKE TELLER'S HANDBOOK; Robert Orben; The
Comedy Center; 801 Wilmington Trust Building, 700 Orange
Street, Wilmington, DE, 19801
THE AD-LIBBER'S HANDBOOK: 2000 New Laughs for
Speakers; Robert Orben; The Comedy Center; 801 Wilming-
ton Trust Building, 700 Orange Street, Wilmington, DE,
19801
THE ENCYCLOPEDIA OF ONE-LINER COMEDY;

Robert Orben; The Comedy Center; 801 Wilmington Trust Building, 700 Orange Street, Wilmington, DE, 19801

DOC BLAKELY'S HANDBOOK OF WIT AND PUNGENT HUMOR; James "Doc" Blakely; Parker Publishing Co., Inc.; West Nyack, NY

PODIUM HUMOR; James Humes; Harper & Row; New York, NY

HOW THE GREAT COMEDY WRITERS CREATE LAUGHTER; Larry Wilde; Nelson-Hall; Chicago, IL

THE GREAT COMEDIANS; Larry Wilde; The Citadel Press; Secaucus, NJ

THE ALGONQUIN WITS; Edited by Robert E. Drennan; The Citadel Press; Secaucus, NJ

HOW SPEAKERS MAKE PEOPLE LAUGH; Bob Bassindale; Parker Publishing Co.; West Nyack, NY

HUMOR POWER; Herb True; Doubleday & Co.; Garden City, NY

A DICTIONARY OF WIT, WISDOM, AND SATIRE; Harper and Row; 10 E. 53rd Street, NY, NY 10022

WHEN IT'S LAUGHTER YOU'RE AFTER; Stewart Harral; Univ. of Okla. Press; Norman, OK

THE PSYCHOLOGY OF HUMOR; Goldstein and McGhee; Academic Press, New York, NY

ENJOYMENT OF LAUGHTER; Max Eastman; Simon and Schuster, New York, NY

THE SENSE OF HUMOR; Max Eastman; Charles Scribner's Sons, New York, NY

HUMOR: Its Origin and Development; McGhee; W. H. Freeman and Co.; San Francisco, CA

Subscription Services

QUOTE; Suite L-100, Piedmont Avenue, N.E., Atlanta, GA 30308

CURRENT COMEDY; Robert Orben; The Comedy Center, Inc., 700 Orange Street, Wilmington, DE 19801

THE SPEECH-MAKER; Mick DeLaney; The Clearing House for Speech Humor, 15259 Wedgewood Station, Seattle, WA 98115

COMEDY and COMMENT; Mack McGinnis, 448 N. Mitchner Avenue, Indianapolis, IN 46219

Cassettes of Humorous Material

General Cassette Corp., 2311 N. 35th Avenue, Box 6940, Phoenix, AZ 85005

Charles W. Jarvis, Box 1094, San Marcos, TX 78666

James "Doc" Blakely, Route 3, P.O. Box 208, Wharton, TX 77488

Robert Henry, Henry Associates, Inc., P.O. Box 1350, Auburn, AL

Jeanne Swanner Robertson, 2905 Forestdale Drive, Burlington, NC 27215

Joe Griffith, P.O. Box 401546, Dallas, TX 75240

Art Holst, 2001 Wilow Knolls Road, Suite 206 WILLOW-BROOK, Peoria, IL 61614

Jansen, Robert H., 7918 Harwood Ave., Wauwatosa, WI 53213

PREACHER: "Do you say your prayers at night, little boy?"
JIMMY: "Yes, sir."
PREACHER: "And do you always say them in the morning, too?"
JIMMY: "No, sir. I ain't scared in the daytime."

Chapter 10

So You've Accepted An Invitation To Speak?

The Audience Asks: "What's in it for me?"

"Oh Lord, fill my mouth with worthwhile stuff and nudge me when I've said enough." That's what I usually say to myself whenever I've been invited to address a group. Assuming you want to be invited back, or to have a group recommend you to others, it's also good advice to remember this observation from an old professional speaker: **"If you want to be seen . . . stand up; if you want to be heard . . . speak up; if you want to be appreciated . . . SHUT UP!"** Putting it another way — BE BRIGHT. BE BRIEF. BE GONE! Obviously, the object of these observations is to avoid boring the members of your audience with a long-winded, dull effort that makes them regret they asked you to speak.

"A speaker has much in common with the captain of a ship," says Robert Orben. "Your listeners are the passengers on this ship. In return for a safe and enjoyable voyage, they voluntarily submit to your expertise, your rules and your leadership. And so, the speaker-skipper has to be in control at all times."

Being in control at all times is a pretty big order but, according to Orben, control begins long before the ship even sails. And he says that when you accept a speaking engagement, try to get as much information as you can about the sponsoring organization, the composition of the audience and the nature of the program. Learn the names of the high-visibility personalities at the head table and something of the group's background and history. Secure the printed program or working agenda. Analyze your position in the program and what's expected of you.

CHECK THE FACILITIES

"Proper Planning Prevents Poor Performance," and how well I know. Certainly a key ingredient to a **superior** performance is making certain that the room facilities are proper **for you!**

I stand six feet two inches tall and invariably I get a lectern that is too short and poorly lit, with a fixed-position microphone that restricts my mobility. I have every right to blame the program chairman, correct? WRONG? I have nobody to blame but myself, because I should check the room arrangements out ahead of time and correct whatever needs correcting. If you start to do a lot of public speaking, you may even find it advisable to carry along your **own** adjustable lectern and one which has a built-in mike and speaker (don't forget a couple of long extension cords).

I've been to a good many public presentations and I would say fully two-thirds are lacking in something. For instance, I attended a conference which had the governor of our state as one of its main participants and here was the meeting facility's situation:

1. An electrical cord was placed in an unsafe location and the very first speaker **tripped** over it on his way to the lectern.

2. The speaker had to check the mike out with the usual "Can you hear me in the back of the room?"

3. Some in the audience had been seated behind pillars, which obstructed their view of the platform.

4. Someone had forgotten to disconnect a phone which was located in the room and several times it rang, much to the consternation of the speakers and the audience.

5. The person who introduced the governor took **four minutes** to do so and in the process, uttered 28 "ahs" and used the word "edification" incorrectly.

Several years ago I made a presentation to a group and I intended to write on a flip chart during my talk. I had a felt-tipped pen with me for making notes on the charts. Would you believe I couldn't get the cap off the pen? Moreover, I didn't have a spare with me so I had to borrow another man's writing instrument — a ball-point pen — but its output didn't have near the visibility at the back of the room.

BLANKETY BLANK BAG

Others have had similar problems. A friend of mine was involved in an award presentation and the lapel pin he was to present was inside a little cellophane bag. And try as he might, he couldn't get the pin out of that little bag. So, he asked for help from another gentleman — and neither could get that pin out of that bag.

Sometime or another, you are bound to be in charge of meeting preparations so I strongly recommend that you "walk through" every situation. Do it from: the viewpoint of the audience, the podium guests, the main speaker. Leave nothing to chance. Test the slide projector, the P.A. system, the light switches, everything. Have a dry run, and then another.

Check the seating arrangements and get members of the audience closer to you, the speaker, and closer to one another. This way you'll have a better chance of getting a ripple effect with your humor and other speech segments. Make sure doors near or beside the head table won't be used after you start your speech. You don't want any distractions.

The conference I mentioned above, which involved the governor, did impress me in at least one way, and that was the appearance by the final speaker of the afternoon. The final speaker was a man. He had the best voice projection. He was the most articulate. He was the best dressed. Overall, he was the most dynamic of them all. He also was **blind**. He couldn't control the speaker's environment, but he certainly knew how to make the best personal presentation. Can't we?

THE FIRST IMPRESSION

A major part of your success might very well be attributable to **your introduction** to the audience. In other words, the build-up you are given by the master of ceremonies or toastmaster is very important for setting the stage for your presentation.

Typically, the emcee will discuss the organization's business, future meetings, and so on and also may tell one or two humorous stories to break the ice and to "warm up" the audience. Often, the story is not very funny but you as the speaker have to sit there, and smile or laugh politely. That's bad enough, but even worse is to have an emcee who is extremely self-conscious and unable to project his or her voice in a clear, self-confident way to properly prepare the way for you.

Not long ago I was sitting at the head table getting ready to speak to an audience of several hundred persons. The microphone was excellent, the room arrangements were superb and we were on an elevated podium, an ideal situation. However, the man next to me leaned over and said somewhat hesitatingly, "I have to introduce you and boy, do I hate this job. I'm really nervous at functions like this."

I tried to reassure him and explained that I and virtually all experienced speakers had butterflies, too, but our own internal nervousness usually doesn't show and that he should just relax and act as if he were talking to one or two friends who really wanted him to succeed.

About five minutes later, he got up to the lectern, fidgeted nervously with his coat and notes, and then proceeded to mumble my name. His words were inaudible to anyone seated more than three feet away. He then glanced at me and sat down, and if the audience hadn't had a printed program, they wouldn't have had the slightest idea who in the world I was.

PREPARE OWN INTRODUCTION

I'm sure that a professional, self-confident introduction by the emcee would have helped considerably and that's why I encourage all speakers to do what they can to control their pre-speech destiny. Specifically, I suggest:

1. Typing out (not hand-writing) your introduction **just the way you want it given.** Send this introduction to the program chairman several days in advance. Furthermore, **carry a duplicate copy with you to your speaking engagement.** On several occasions I have arrived at the engagement only to find that the chairman or emcee had been changed at the last moment and the current emcee had not received the typed introduction. The duplicate copy solved the problem.

Also, if your name is rather difficult to pronounce (as mine is with many people) I recommend that you spell your name out phonetically in the introduction and make a point of pronouncing it correctly to the emcee. For example, the name Isaacson can be presented as EYE-ZIK-SUN.

2. Telling the emcee that you would appreciate it very much if he or she didn't deviate from the typed copy. One other time I gave my typed introduction to an emcee who was a personal friend and he thought he was doing me a favor by ignoring it completely and telling the audience what a great guy I was and what an enjoyable friendship we had had over the years. The trouble was, **the audience never did learn what my qualifica-**

tions were for addressing them.

3. It's okay to build yourself up in the introduction, particularly where qualifications are concerned, but it's also a good idea to cut yourself down to the audience's size. One of the most effective introductions I ever heard was made by Nick Carter of the Nightingale-Conant Corporation, who was emceeing a conference I attended. He gave a long list of the speaker's qualifications, commented about the college degrees the speaker had earned, and cited the numerous articles the speaker had published in his area of expertise. After this glowing intro, Nick then said, "He also has a note from his mommy!" The audience roared and the speaker had been beautifully presented.

4. Another important thing to do, although a rather touchy one, is to try to get the organization's planning or meeting director **to assign an introducer who has the proper qualifications,** that is, someone who will lay the proper groundwork for your presentation. You might suggest something like this, "Mr. Smith, I know that you want a successful meeting and one way that we can guarantee a good reception and a good response to me as your speaker is by choosing someone to introduce me who is a self-confident person, who is well liked and someone who knows how to keep the introduction short. Can you sugggest someone like that?"

DON'T FORGET TO LISTEN

As mentioned earlier, many after-dinner speeches are preceded by a group's business meeting and it's easy to let your mind drift or to be thinking about your upcoming message to those assembled. I would suggest, though, that you listen rather carefully to what's going on in case you later want to make reference to a particular point in your speech or in case the emcee has made some remark about you of which you need to be aware. If you are daydreaming, you might miss a valuable piece of information.

I was guilty of that on one occasion. The emcee was telling about another member of their organization who had been hospitalized with ulcers. I got up a few minutes later, not having paid any attention to the emcee's earlier remarks, and I launched into my speech about positive thinking. Farther into my speech, I commented that I once had had ulcers and "it's not what you eat, that causes ulcers, it's what eats you." It dawned on me later that this might have been a direct (and negative) reflection on their fellow member. If I had been paying better attention earlier, I could have skipped right over this ulcer reference and could have made some other point.

There's an old proverb that says, "Speaking without thinking is shooting without taking aim." I was guilty of not taking aim.

I might add that listening can be as important as speaking, whether you are a speaker about to assume control of the lectern or whether you are someone in the audience. N. Donald Edwards, who operates a learning center in Stanford, Connecticut and is a consultant to business, says in a recent article in *"The Typographer,"* "We've ended up as a society with a 25% listening effectiveness factor. That means 75% of communications is virtually misunderstood . . . . Put me with any sales organization for an hour and I'll tell you who the best producers are because they also turn out to be the best listeners."

LISTENING REQUIRES EFFORT

Robert Conklin, in his book, *"How to Get People to Do Things,"* says "Listening is loving." He adds, "Of all of the actions that can make another human being feel significant and worthwhile there is none more vital than skilled listening. Still, it is the most overlooked." He goes on to say that it has been his experience in public teaching that everyone wanted to learn how to talk but no one wanted to learn how to listen.

He says that in order to become a better listener, you've got to make the effort. He cites the example of your listening to a lecture on how to pack a parachute and how you might find it quite dull. However, if you were told that the next day you would be expected to pack your own chute and then jump from an airplane, you obviously would become a much better listener in the first place.

One of the best definitions I ever saw of listening was given by a youngster in a high school class in music appreciation. When the teacher asked what the difference is between listening and hearing, a hand went up and a student offered this: "Listening is **wanting** to hear!"

Someone else has said, "Listening requires that we listen not only with the ear and the eye but with the mind and heart."

In her book *"How to Get Whatever You Want Out of Life"*, Dr. Joyce Brothers says that listening, not imitation, may be the sincerest form of flattery and that most people don't listen but rather simply wait out another person's speech or comment, planning just what they are going to say when he stops talking.

DON'T UNDERESTIMATE YOUR AUDIENCE

Earl Nightingale is a source of stimulating material as well as wisdom, particularly where audiences are concerned. He says, "Never underestimate your audience — no matter who you are or how successful you are. Before you make a speech, think about the group you're going to speak to. Chances are it includes some very successful people."

Do not, he adds, talk "down" to an audience but rather stretch them (without being patronizing). He says an audience will usually love you if you over-estimate their knowledge and understanding of your subject. But he admonishes, "Never, never, ever, under any circumstances, sell your audience short. Never underestimate their brains nor their ability to grasp what you're talking about."

The bottom line? **It pays to know your audience!**

My friend Dr. Lou Wolter would agree with that. Whether it's advertising (his specialty at Drake University) or public speaking (he does a great deal of that), he would be the first to tell you that you indeed must know your audience. "People don't want a quarter-inch drill," he says, "they want a quarter-inch hole." It follows logically that audiences don't want just a speaker — they want the **benefits** that a speaker can give them.

An audience certainly doesn't want a nervous speaker because listeners will be distracted and won't know what the benefits are in the message.

Nightingale asserts, "Every speaker of quality, I believe, suffers from nervousness before a speech — the degree of it depending upon the audience he's to face."

LOVE FOR AUDIENCE

He continues, "I find it helps me a great deal if I can develop a kind of love for the audience before I begin to talk. By love, I mean a feeling of agape, which, originally, meant a feeling of love between Christians — but which can certainly include all people regardless of their religious leanings. The feeling I like to develop for a speech is a feeling of brotherhood. After all, we belong to the same club — the same species. Our humanity is our membership card."

I would echo Nightingale's further statement that most people are nice people. They want the same things you or I want and they want to enjoy your speech. Indeed, there is no reason in the world to be fearful or to consider the listeners hostile toward you. They want you to succeed!

By making the proper preparations for your speech, by checking the facilities, getting the right introduction prepared and being certain to listen and not underestimating your audience, you now are ready to **involve** your audience.

INVOLVE AND COMPLIMENT

Cavett Robert tells us . . .
　　Our audience sits there
　　Like owls in a tree.
　　They're silently yelling . . .
　　"WHAT'S IN IT FOR ME?"

The consensus of opinion among professional speakers is that it's extremely important to involve your audience in order to maintain their interest in you and in your subject matter. How can this be done? There are many ways.

My friend Art (Mr. Lucky) Fettig shared with me several

approaches, such as:

> Getting your audience to join with you in applauding something or someone.
> Complimenting your audience with sincerity.
> Asking your audience a question.
> Physically "invading" the territory of your audience.

Art goes into much greater detail in his excellent book *"How to Hold An Audience in the Hollow of Your Hand."* I can recommend it highly.

At the beginning of one recent speech, I thanked the emcee for his fine introduction and then I asked the audience to join me in a round of applause for the emcee and their board of directors. The audience responded enthusiastically and it helped to get them in a better frame of mind for my presentation.

Other speakers believe, as Art does, that it's also a good idea to compliment the audience. For example, you could say "I know that most of you have a great deal of knowledge on this subject but your very presence here tonight shows that you are keeping your minds open to the possibility of picking up an additional tip or two from me on how you might increase your sales and expand your markets."

Still others will start by saying something like, "How many persons here have ever experienced a sales slump but didn't know what caused it?" Or, they might ask, "Let me see a show of hands of those who are interested in increasing sales during the next six months." Any number of questions could be asked to get the audience involved.

Many speakers like to "invade" the territory of their audience. That is easily done if you arrange beforehand for a mike attached to a long cord. By wandering into their midst, you will generate a great deal of interest and alertness.

These and other audience-involvement ideas can help to build rapport between the speaker and listeners and will help you put your message across with maximum effect. The audience's participation will help to answer the question,

"WHAT'S IN IT FOR ME?"

HOW IMPORTANT IS THE WAY I DRESS?

Are physical appearance, dress and grooming important when it comes to oral communications? They are if you want to have your ideas more readily accepted by the audience, according to studies that have been made.

It has been found that physical attractiveness does play an influential role. And I don't mean the degree of handsomeness or beauty of the speaker but rather the speaker's "package."

Your clothing style, for instance, can speak almost as loudly as your message. And I would ask you this question: How can you be perceived as an expert on your subject if you aren't astute enough to physically present yourself well?

You need to be as contemporary in your appearance as you are with your message. There are books available on "dressing for success" and I strongly recommend that you read them.

You may be a shirt-sleeve presenter at meetings in your office but for outside presentations you definitely need to wear a coat if you are a male and a coat or appropriate dress if you are a female. Polish your shoes, wear conservative colors and make sure your shirts or blouses are in the current style. Out-of-style clothing and wrinkled collars mark you as a person who is behind the times.

APPEARANCE A FORM OF LANGUAGE

Odd, isn't it, the way many people invest in expensive homes and cars to project an image of success — but they don't expend the effort necessary to improve their **personal** image.

Writing in a recent issue of *Gentlemen's Quarterly,* Michael R. Solomon commented, "Our appearance can also be considered a form of language, in the sense that it expresses or communicates something about us. Individual garments serve as the words that are combined in various ways to create 'sentences.' Just as a word's meaning is often dependent on the sentence in which it appears (and can be distorted if taken out of context), apparel 'words' rely on the other 'words' with which they're combined. For clothes to communicate, they must be assembled into a coherent whole, so their overall silhouette and coordination will render them meaningful for the roles we play.

"That particular visual message often takes precedence over the other signals we send out or receive. Although the messages are occasionally contradictory, we tend to place more credence in the visual one."

He continues, "Effective communication is a paramount goal. At times, flexibility is necessary in constructing the messages we send to ensure that they're properly understood by those on the receiving end."

GETTING AN HONEST CRITIQUE

In order to measure one's progress, it's necessary to be "graded," or critiqued. It's difficult to get a truly honest critique from members of the audience because most people hate to be terribly blunt or candid about your speech. Frequently, at the conclusion, a speaker will hear comments like "Nice job," "Good message," or "I really enjoyed your talk."

But if you want to grow as a speaker, you also need to hear constructive criticism. Maybe your speech lacked continuity, or you had poor eye contact, or talked in a monotone, or you belabored a point when it wasn't necessary. Because you seldom will get a realistic appraisal of your performance, I strongly recommend that you tape all of your speeches. Play back your tapes several times to see if you can detect where some part of your talk could be shortened or improved through re-wording, or where changes could be made in vocal variety, and so on.

Columnist Sydney Harris writes that at the height of W. S. Gilbert's success, when the Gilbert and Sullivan operettas had standing room only in London, Gilbert appeared on the witness stand in a libel case. He was asked by the defense attorney whether he had read the many compliments paid to him by a certain magazine. Gilbert replied: "I never read favorable criticisms. I prefer reading unfavorable ones. I know how good I am, but I do not know how bad I am."

As public speakers, we, too, may know how good we are but perhaps we don't know how bad we are, and that's the value of an honest critique.

A thorough evaluation of your speeches is another good reason why participation in a Toastmaster club is such a valuable experience. Club members are virtually mandated to tell you through an evaluation process what they feel were the strengths **and** weaknesses of your effort.

Someone has said that "failures are inevitable — not insurmountable." I agree. To that I would add, "You can fail without being a failure." You will be more proud of some speeches than of others, the same way some baseball players perform better in certain games than others. No one hits a home run every time at bat.

Just keep in mind what Bob Orben said at the top of this chapter about a speaker having much in common with the captain of a ship. Your listeners are the passengers on this ship. **It need not be the Titanic.**

———

"One big bar in the mental tiger cage is called *Fear of Failure*. Nothing blocks dynamic creativity more than such a fear. Why? Because a fear of failure is really a fear of embarrassment. The need for self-esteem is one of the deepest of all human needs. To expose our self-dignity to the hazard of public ridicule is a risk we instinctively avoid! Our inclination is to play it safe and avoid the possibility of a disgrace by not even trying. Work this confirming, negative concept loose from your thinking. Here's the way. Remember that not failure but low aim is the crime."

ROBERT H. SCHULLER
You Can Become the Person You Want to Be

Creed For American Speech

With the ancients I believe that as a man speaks, so is he. Therefore will I live aware of my world: having a listening ear, a seeing eye, an understanding heart, and an expressive tongue. I will pay as much attention to my address as to my dress, for words are power. I acknowledge them to be the flowering of the mind, the mesage of the heart, the ambassadors of the soul. Since I am an American, I pledge my speech in The American Language . . . in all its strength, beauty, and simplicity. Nor will I be guilty of speaking idle words, guarding my tongue as a door unto a treasure-house wherein dwells wisdom bought with knowledge and experience, tolerance purchased by failures, compassion paid for dearly out of suffering. Therefore, if I speak at all, I will speak clearly and in good taste, simply and effectively, in the correct use of our mother tongue.

ELISABETH FERGUSON von HESSE
SO TO SPEAK
J.B. Lippincott Company

Chapter 11

Speak Professionally — And Get Paid!

"Money is not the root of all evil."

Someone has said, "What's worth doing is worth doing for money." That's a good point and one that certainly can apply to public speaking.

There are a lot of speakers around who have annual earnings from public speaking that are in six figures. We naturally expect famous personalities and internationally-known politicians to receive high fees, i.e., $10,000 to $20,000 per speech, but I know of a number of professionals who have a very nice income earning anywhere from $500 to $2,500 per speech —

and they are in demand!

How can YOU command those fees? Cavett Robert, one of the very best, says it's imperative that you "learn to do something extremely well and then get a message developed that's crying for expression." He adds, "then take three or four years and learn how to really communicate. Get a compulsion to help other people and speak from the heart — not the mind."

Three or four years sound like a long time, don't they? Says Cavett, "If it were easy, everyone would be doing it. The difficulty lies in the opportunity. If you can believe strongly in what you are doing, you'll succeed."

HOW MUCH SHOULD I CHARGE?

How does one start on the pathway to professional speaking? If you are like my friends Larry Huegli, Wayne Humphreys, John Curoe and Chuck Knodle (all professionals and darned good ones), you start by giving a heck of a lot of **free** talks — to scouting groups, Chambers of Commerce, local civic associations and church organizations. From there, it all depends on you as an individual. In the early stages, of course, some program chairpersons will offer a very, very small "honorarium" plus travel expenses, if you're lucky. These honoraria range from $10 to $50 or so. As your reputation grows, it won't be long before organizations with larger budgets start knocking at your door.

You'll frequently agonize over whether to accept a $100 speaking engagement when you know you're worth a lot more, and perhaps have been receiving a lot more. Whether to accept a low fee or not depends on a lot of things, including time, distance and the specific audience. A low fee might not be too bad if in the process you expose your speaking talents to a lot of people who may be in a position to hire you later on in your professional career.

As of this writing, most of the professionals I work with on a statewide basis request and get anywhere from $350 to $500, plus expenses. Nationally-known speakers on the speaking "circuit" are available for around $2,000 and up, plus expenses. The super famous (former U.S. Secretaries of State, etc.) receive $10,000 and up.

Larry Huegli, whom I mentioned earlier in this chapter, was a professional broadcaster before he started speaking professionally and this no doubt gave him an edge in the confidence department but he, too, had to struggle to make a name for himself. He shared some insights and observations with me about professional speaking.

LOCAL, REGIONAL, OR NATIONAL?

There are, says Larry, basically three types of professional speakers — local, regional and national. The "local" speaker is normally one who is just starting in the speak-for-a-fee field. He or she usually confines appearances to a local radius of 50 to 60 miles and charges between $100 and $200 per speech.

The "regional" speaker normally has several years' experience and stays within his or her own state or region of the country. He or she, like the local speaker, has a full-time job and has spent a few years in the field of speaking but still must rely on that full-time job to earn a livelihood. This type of speaker can usually go to-and-from a speaking assignment within a few hours. The regional speaker is, usually, more in demand than a local speaker and the fees charged can range from $350 to $750.

The "national" speaker, as the name implies, travels all over the country delivering speeches and can command a relatively large fee and the size of the fee depends on the "name" recognition of the individual involved. Just because a speaker is a full-time national speaker doesn't necessarily mean he or she is a superior speaker. Because someone charges a hefty fee, many program chairpersons think that person is "better" than someone who charges from $350 to $750 per speech. Often the higher fee is charged not so much because of the talent but rather because of the expense.

The full-time national speaker traveling the country generally has a full-time secretary, an answering service and high telephone and advertising bills, which require a large fee to pay the expenses. On the other hand, the local or regional speaker normally does all the "secretarial" and other duties without a full-time staff person to assist, resulting in low overhead.

As an example, a local or regional speaker must type up his or her mailings, design the advertising brochure, fold and stuff the brochures into envelopes, seal the envelopes, lick the stamps, arrange for a mailing permit (if bulk service is used) and then mail. It is a time-consuming job that must be done by the speaker.

Larry told me that a recent mailing he made of 100 brochures took him five hours to complete from start to finish. Then, to top things off, it is discouraging, he says, to know that most mailings are thrown away without even so much as a peek. One national program planner recently told him that he receives "thousands" of these types of mailings and doesn't even look at them! He just throws them into the circular file.

AVERAGE RETURN IS TWO PERCENT

The national average for a return on mailouts is about one to two percent and a recent mailing of 600 of Larry's brochures proved that point! He received only FOUR inquiries out of 600 and only booked one! Professional speaking isn't the simple, easy, high-paying job it appears to be! In addition to those problems, a speaker must also obtain a list of prospective "planners," such as local club presidents or association presidents. Many times such groups will not allow the names of their presidents or members to be released. There are groups that you can purchase such names from. However, the local or regional speaker can't always afford those services.

Here are additional observations from Larry:
"It may be hard and cold but I have learned that a speaker's success depends a great deal on the program planner — not the audience he or she addresses. Granted, many speeches are booked by people who have heard you. However, there are many speeches booked through the mailout method. Please keep in mind that prospective planners have no way of knowing the ability of a speaker unless they contact a previous

planner who has hired you for a speech. It is there that a speaker 'lives or dies'. No matter how good (or bad) your speech was, it is all up to the planner.

"Take a recent example: One November I was asked to speak to a conference of plumbing/wholesalers from a six-state region. The morning I was to speak I developed a high fever and a bad cold. I should have remained in bed. However, the group would have been left without a speaker. In spite of my condition I attended the conference (120 miles away) and did my motivational speech. Because of my physical condition, I couldn't get motivated, but I did the best I could. While it wasn't my best speech ever, I thought I had done a good job.

"I later learned that those who had heard me that night kept quoting me and my speech during the workshops the next day! This was an indication that the audience listened and, apparently, liked and agreed with what I said. The planner said she would consider me for future conferences but obviously was not that personally pleased with my performance, for whatever reason.

LOST BOOKINGS

"Eight months later, I was contacted by another planner to give TWO national convention speeches because of a recommendation from one of the members of an organization he represented. He, verbally, asked me to set the two dates aside and said he would write me a letter a week later confirming my appearances. In the meantime, as luck would have it, he contacted the planner for the plumbing supply wholesalers conference who told him that **she** would not have me back, but said I was 'O.K.' As a result, my appearances at the two national conventions were cancelled. Also, I lost a thousand dollars' worth of bookings. The person who called for the recommendation had no choice, however. The plumbing planner didn't like my speech even though I was apparently well accepted by the audience that night since they quoted me often the next day!

"It is nice to please your audience but you had better also please the person who hired you or forget any references in the future!"

Many times a program planner will specifically ask for a certain type of speech — humorous, motivational, inspirational, and so on. However, the planner doesn't always know the mood of the audience. Recently Larry gave a speech at an awards dinner for a blue collar manufacturing group. All were "on-line" production workers and Larry was asked to give an all-humorous presentation. Thinking the planner knew her audience, he relied on her judgment and went to the speech with nothing but humorous speech notes.

WHEN HUMOR BOMBS

His humor did not fly that night (probably helped along by a 90-minute "happy hour") and he bombed. The feeling was so overwhelming that he has never been caught in that trap again. All of his speeches, generally, have the same opening — about 15 minutes of humor — and then he goes into the main portion of his speech. Under this format, he can use his all-humorous speech, his motivational presentation or his humorous/inspirational speech. If while he is giving his "humor" he learns the audience doesn't like his style of funnies, he will change after the opening and go into one of his more serious speeches. To be completely safe he always takes **two** speeches to the lectern with him — and he says he never has been in trouble since.

John Curoe also started out giving freebies while farming and selling real estate on the side. He now is virtually a full-time professional speaker and has had the rare experience of having some of his clients pay him **more** than his normal fee because they liked him so much.

John firmly believes in soliciting help from experts in the speaking field and as a member of the National Speakers Association, has received valuable assistance from other members on such things as speaking style, the use of humor and the preparation of a personal brochure.

EXPECT THE UNEXPECTED

Certainly one good piece of advice is to **expect the unexpected** when you arrive someplace to speak. I remember showing up for a television interview on the subject of public speaking and the interviewer told me — AFTER I arrived — that she would appreciate it if I could be "on camera" TWICE AS LONG AS ORIGINALLY SCHEDULED because another guest had failed to appear. Moreover, after we were into the on-camera interview, I learned to my dismay that she was deviating from a previously agreed to set of questions. The lesson to be learned here is: Be prepared . . . AND THEN SOME!

Another time I was scheduled to be an after-dinner speaker and during the course of the dinner, the waitress spilled prime rib juice over the front of my trousers. It was an accident but it forced me to hide behind the lectern throughout my talk. Going to and from the lectern, I held my hands awkwardly in front of me to screen the big wet spot on the front of my trousers.

John recalls a time when he slipped getting out of his car and the fall ripped the crotch of his trousers from stem to stern. This occurred just minutes before his speech. What did he do? He went on with the show, but confessed that he kept his legs together throughout dinner and throughout the speech.

TIPS ON A PERSONAL BROCHURE

For prospective clients who never have heard you before, one important way to get their attention is to have a professional-looking personal brochure.

While there is no substitute for having a good message and excellent delivery, a brochure **can help** you get your foot in some doorways. Here are some significant points to remember relative to the preparation of your brochure:

1. Don't write it yourself unless you have lots of experience as a copywriter and/or graphics artist. If you are an amateur, your finished product will look amateurish. Spend a few bucks to do the job right.

2. By all means use a photograph (a head shot or a shot of you in front of a happy audience) but again, use a professional person to take the pictures.

3. Don't skimp on the quality of the printing or the quality of the paper. Engage a commercial typesetter to prepare a good-looking finished piece instead of using copy from a typewriter.

4. Make sure the finished printed piece will fold nicely into a Number 10 (standard business size) mailing envelope. Color co-ordinate your mailing envelope with your brochure to give it an added touch of professionalism.

5. List past audiences you have addressed and quote the better written responses you have received, i.e., testimonial letters.

6. If your education and job experience are impressive, reflect that information, too.

7. If you have received some special award or are an author with publications to your credit, tell about them.

8. Do not indicate what your **fee** is for speaking. Keep that negotiable and base it on size of audience, length of your speech and the size of your client's budget.

ANALYZING THE MARKET

Someone has studied this meeting- and convention-prone country of ours and discovered that there is something like an average of 100,000 meetings weekly in the U.S. and each requires one or more speakers. Even during a downturn in the economy, the number of conferences does not seem to diminish appreciably. If anything, the number may **increase** because businesses need to motivate their staffs even more aggressively in order to survive. Moreover, state, regional and national meetings continue to be important social and educational diversions for participants and these meetings serve to reward employees for a job well done.

When you are ready to step beyond the speak-for-free stage, one of the first things I would do is to obtain directories of all the trade, manufacturing and nonprofit associations in your state. Send them a copy of your brochure — not once, but several times over the first two years. If response is minimal, start calling them on the telephone and ask them what it takes to be scheduled as a speaker at their next convention.

If your budget permits, run an ad in the yellow pages of your local telephone directory under "Public Speaking." I ran such an ad and had no response for about the first six months. Since then, I regularly receive calls and the fees I have collected more than pay for the ad. I'm also able to schedule **other** speakers (for a fee, of course).

Send a news release to your local newspaper to announce that you have started a professional speaking business.

Make a cassette tape recording of your speeches and duplicate the best one to send to prospects. The cost of tapes has come down dramatically in recent times and it's relatively easy to duplicate them by borrowing someone else's tape player and connecting theirs to yours via an inexpensive interfacing cord, which you can obtain from your local electronics supply house.

ENTERTAINING AN AUDIENCE

Twice a year, the National Speakers Association conducts seminars for its members and the typical session is led by one or more of the Association's outstanding members. One such session was chaired by **Grady Robinson,** another fine humorist. He offers this advice about professional speaking:

"Humor is your key to making money in this business. You have to have entertainment value in your program, whether you are a trainer, a real estate person — whatever you do — you've got to have some entertainment value, you've got to have some uplift, some happiness and have a program that is so good that when the people walk out the back door they pat you on the back and the meeting planner gets a pat on the back for having you there and making them feel so good.

"So humor may be the absolute most important thing in all of this business. It may not be the most important thing in communications, it may not be the most important thing in politics and religion but if you're going to sell your services and make a living at being a speaker, humor just may be the most important thing.

"What makes people laugh? Something funny. What's funny? What's involved? THE SPEAKER...THE MATERIAL...THE AUDIENCE (or the occasion, the event).

"Which of the three do you think is the most important? I THINK THE AUDIENCE IS THE MOST IMPORTANT OF THE THREE. HERE'S WHY: Some places you can get up and deliver the best humorous material in the world and only get a whimper from the audience. Some places you get up and **everything** you do gets a roar.

"The second most important thing is the speaker. The material is third. Furthermore, you need to develop a "character" to fit your type of presentation. A stance.

"The stance from which you approach humor is very important. My stance is 'Arkansas.' Jeannie Robertson does 'tall' humor. Jack Benny was a cheapo. Rodney Dangerfield gets no respect. You have to have a stance from which you do your humor. You can't grab a joke from Brooklyn, do a drug joke from L.A., do a dirty joke from Chicago, do a southern joke and then throw all of that into a package and think you're going to be a humorist. You have to have a character from which to fit your material in.

"What is laughter? The punch line is a surprise. A mental train wreck. **We laugh at the tragedies, the injustices, the absurdities and craziness of life.**

"The funniest things that you can tell are the embarrassing things that have happened to you. Lost luggage, getting on the wrong airplane, winding up in the wrong city, these are the things people will laugh at the most. These are things people will laugh at removed by time and space.

"You must have a willingness to play the fool. If you are going to get up to do humor you are going to have to bring the facade down and be willing to be laughed at. Some people cannot really act goofy on the stage and do body movements or make facial expressions that need to be made because they just can't get loose and they're afraid somebody's going to laugh at them.

"Some people can't get the child out, they can't get the clown out, because they are so sophisticated. People with a strong self-image are not afraid to be laughed at. You gotta have a commitment to humor.

"Be careful about taking a joke from a joke book and using it on the stage. What may be funny in **written** form may bomb when told from the stage.

"How do we create material?

"Gather suitable material from books and life situations. Create the proper atmosphere. Do your own thing. Relate to the audience, and not the material. Use the fewest words possible when telling your humor.

"The most important thing to comedy? TIMING. Allow the audience to laugh. Stand there and wait a minute . . . allow them to laugh. Stand up, take command, create the proper atmosphere.

"Tell a story from your **own** experience. Do not try to make up a story. Close with a punch line and be sure to polish the story.

"You can learn to do humor, like hitting a golf ball. You can learn to do it well and become a humorist.

"Fame and tranquility can never be bedfellows."
                                                            MONTAIGNE

"Hide not your talents, they for use were made.
What's a sun-dial in the shade?"

BENJAMIN FRANKLIN

"We might ask ourselves: How much am I worth if I have
nothing except myself? Self-esteem is the way we tend to
indicate our personal evaluation of ourselves. It's expressed in
confidence and the willingness to try new things and move
without fear into the future."

EARL NIGHTINGALE

"I always believe where I'm going is so much more exciting
than where I've been."

DELLA REESE

Only Three Criticisms

The late Senator Alben W. Barkley told the story of
how he had used a manuscript, instead of notes, for
a speech. After he sat down, he turned to a friend
and asked, "What did you think of it?" "Well," came
the answer, "I have only three criticisms. First, you
read it. Second, you read it poorly. Third, it wasn't
worth reading."

Chapter 12

Personal Fulfillment Through Speaking

"May you live all the days of your life."

I attended one of Zig Ziglar's seminars recently and I especially liked his definition of success, which was as follows: *"Success is what you have done compared to what you are capable of doing."*

If you want to become a better public speaker, I believe you can. But you must want to and you must honestly ask yourself: "What am I capable of doing?"

Zig says what you are and where you are is because of what you put into your mind. He sprinkles that phrase throughout his talk. *What you are and where you are is because of what you put into your mind.*

To dramatize that point, he asked the audience, which numbered several thousand persons, to call out to him the words that best describe the attributes of someone who is **successful**. Zig wrote on the blackboard the words the audience flung at him and here they are:

Honest
Enthusiastic
Faithful
Persistent
Positive
High self-esteem
High personal values
Confident
Good listener
Integrity
Empathic
Ambitious
Caring
Disciplined
Goal Seeking
Patient
Loyal
Prideful
Creative
Inspiring
Visionary
Commitment
Hard Worker
Sense of Humor

Study this list again. Did you notice anything? Are words like "rich," "wealthy," "famous," conspicuous by their absence? Almost all of these words listed, according to Zig, ARE THE RESULT OF **ATTITUDE** AND NOT SKILL.

If you truly want to be a better oral communicator — whether for personal enrichment, job promotion, or ego —

then cultivate the right attitude to reach that objective. As Thomas Huxley observed, "Perhaps the most valuable result of all education is the ability to make yourself do the thing you have to do, when it ought to be done, whether you like it or not. This is the first lesson to be learned."

Perhaps you think you are too old to tackle the challenge of public speaking. Don't forget that Cavett Robert didn't start speaking as a professional until he was 60. It's too bad that so many people look at a certain age as a limitation. We all slow down, physically, as we get older but we need not be held back in other areas of our existence.

NOTHING IS TOO LATE

Let me remind you of Longfellow's observations on the virtues of growing old:

> It is too late! Ah, nothing is too late
> Till the tired heart shall cease to palpitate.
> Cato learned Greek at eighty; Sophocles
> Wrote his grand Oedipus, and Simonides
> Bore off the prize of verse from his compeers,
> When each had numbered more than four score years;
> Chaucer at Woodstock with the nightingales,
> At sixty wrote the Canterbury Tales;
> Goethe at Weimar, toiling to the last,
> Completed Faust when eighty years were past.
> These are indeed exceptions; but they show
> How far the gulf stream of our youth may flow
> Into the Arctic regions of our lives . . .
> For age is opportunity no less
> Than youth itself, though in another dress,
> And as the evening twilight fades away
> The sky is filled with stars, invisible by day.

MORE SELF-RESPECT

There will be setbacks along the way, regardless of your age. I still can recall my first feeble attempts at speaking in public. They are painful memories, in some respects, but in other respects they have enabled me to have more self-respect. Harry

Emerson Fosdick said, "Happiness is not mostly pleasure; it is mostly victory." In my speaking efforts, I guess I've had a lot of happiness that I wouldn't have had otherwise.

Some years ago, when the champion gymnast Cathy Rigby failed to achieve some of her Olympic goals, her mother said to her, "Cathy, doing your best is more important than being the best." I believe that's good advice for speakers, too.

One of my favorite all-time public speakers was the Reverend Bishop Fulton Sheen. This is what he told one audience: "Applause sums up the highest of Christian virtues. To applaud, as you just did, at the beginning of the speech, is an act of faith. If you applaud in the middle of my speech, it is an act of hope. And if you applaud at the end of my speech, it is an act of charity."

Like Bishop Sheen, I've experienced a number of acts of charity but they have sustained me through thick and thin and have given me the necessary impetus to go forward.

COMMUNICATION, THE KEY TO UNDERSTANDING

A number of years ago, Canadian businessman Sir William Maxwell Aitken asserted that every person who wished to be successful in business should learn to speak in public. I maintain that if you wish to be successful in anything, you should learn to speak in public. Why? Because, how can you not communicate? So if you have to communicate orally, why not hone that skill to the sharpest possible edge?

Sir William said that the person who cannot express ideas clearly and confidently may be compared to an athlete who goes to the track with shoes that pinch. In other words, the athlete has a disability — a needless disability.

It may sound a little melodramatic, but Jonathan Swift said, "May you live all the days of your life." Submitting to your fear of public speaking is **not** living — it's merely existing in a world that's crying out for better communication at all levels of human endeavor.

Dr. Philip G. Zimbardo, whose book on shyness is mentioned in Chapter 3, issues this challenge: "If you have but one life to live, live it with high self-esteem! It is your choice, a decision not made in the heavens but in your head."

I firmly believe you can achieve personal fulfillment not only by hearing applause but also in the struggle on the way to the arena. Because when we call on that intangible thing called "our higher selves," we really experience something beautiful. The Second Century philosopher Epictetus said it so well:

> *When you have shut your doors and darkened your room, remember, never to say that you are alone; for you are not alone, but God is within and your genius is within.*

My speech mentor, Sam Zickefoose, says that effective public speaking is Nature's way to develop personality. "I believe this tool is available to all speakers," adds Sam, "and as we all know, a good workman is known by the finest tools — it therefore behooves us to use the finest tools in this elusive task of building our own personality. We cannot, we must not settle for less."

Sam shared with me the story of a wealthy man who called his servant in and told him that he was leaving the country for a year and that while he was gone, he wanted the servant to build him a new house. The wealthy man told him to build it well, and that when he returned, he would pay all the bills for material and for his labor.

". . . THE REST OF YOUR LIFE"

Shortly after the employer left, the servant decided that he was foolish to work so hard, so he started cutting corners and squandering the money he saved. When his master came back, he said after paying all the bills, "Are you satisfied with the house?" When the servant said that he was, the master said, "Good, because it is yours. You can live in it the rest of your life."

Concludes Sam, "The Creator has provided **us** with the material and the finest tools, but it is up to us to build our own personalities. Are you satisfied with the one you are going to live in the rest of your life?"

Somerset Maugham said, "It's a funny thing about life ... if you refuse to accept anything but the best, you very often get it."

One whom Maugham admired was England's famous naval hero — Lord Nelson. Nelson suffered from — of all things — seasickness throughout his entire life. Needless to say, the man who destroyed Napoleon's fleet did not let it interfere with his career. He not only learned to live with his personal weakness, he conquered it. Most of us have our own personal "seasickness," too. For some it may be physical, for others psychological. Usually, it is a personal, private struggle, carried on quietly within ourselves. No one will pin a medal on us for winning it, but nothing can dim the satisfaction of knowing we did not surrender.

THE TEST OF OUR HUMANITY

Earl Nightingale says, "It is wisely said that before we can do something, we must be something. It is not what we *have,* but what we *are* that makes the difference. Dr. Eva Brann of St. John's College at Annapolis, Maryland put it marvelously well in a Commencement Address. She said, 'The test of our humanity is what we settle for.'

"When we walk to the lectern before a group of our peers, many of whom are wise, very intelligent people, it is soon apparent to them what we have settled for. Our audience knows whether we run deep or shallow, whether we truly believe in what we're saying, or are attempting to patronize and placate or pull the wool over the eyes of those in attendance.

"How do we motivate an audience? We become motivating people through our own growth, knowledge and interest in our subject and the audience ... through our integrity!"

A SENSE OF FULFILLMENT

Some years ago, Dr. Monroe Markley wrote a poem that seems most appropriate for those of us who work hard to become effective public speakers. It goes like this:

The men who are unsatisfied,
They are the ones who lead.
They force humanity ahead
By strident word and deed.

They bring us out by bygone ways;
They guide us through the dark
To where some man *unsatisfied* . . .
Has set a shining mark.

I know of no better way to communicate your knowledge, your integrity or your dissatisfaction with mediocrity than through public speaking. Moreover, you will gain a tremendous sense of personal fulfillment through your public speaking efforts.

I feel especially fulfilled with **my** public speaking whenever anyone comes up to me after the speech and says, "Max, you made us laugh, cry and think."

I feel fulfilled when someone comes up to me after a speech and asks for a quotation in my speech that moved them.

I feel fulfilled when someone contacts me days later and says, "Max, I loved your humorous stories. Would you write them down for me?"

I feel fulfilled if I have helped a beginning speaker to see the possibilities that lie ahead.

I feel fulfilled when I think I have lifted someone who is down spiritually.

I feel fulfilled when I think of Cavett Robert's assertion that "The greatest ministry in the world is helping other people. Anybody who is teaching other people to live more abundantly is doing the work of God."

I feel fulfilled whenever I recall what one of my sons told me several years ago after I had delivered a talk. He said "Dad, that was great!"

COUNTLESS MARKS

I feel fulfilled whenever I read the following poem and

consider the influence that is mine to share:

> My life shall touch a dozen lives
> Before this day is done,
> Leave countless marks for good or ill
> Ere sets the evening sun;

> This is the wish I always make,
> The prayer I always pray:
> Lord, may my life help other lives
> It touches by the way.

My friends, YOU can leave countless marks for good if you use your speaking ability in positive ways. YOU, too, can feel fulfilled by commencing now to embellish your public speaking skills to the full measure of your ability.

Let me close with this advice from John Cardinal Newman:

> **"Fear not that thy life shall come to an end,**
> **but rather fear that it shall never have a beginning."**

APPENDIX

While preparing this book, I had several opportunities to speak to various groups.

One in particular especially impressed me — it was a group of people representing their telephone company's Speakers Bureau. I talked to them about the opportunity that we all have to become better oral communicators and I complimented them on the efforts they were making.

At the conclusion of my talk, I asked them to share with me how **they** managed to control **their** fears of public speaking. Here's what they told me:

"Put your fears in the back seat. No matter how public a person you become, we all admit that fear is with us. Recognize it, use it as a tool to get you on 'high' to become sharp and ready as well as prepared."

David Callahan

"When speaking to a large audience, you may overcome fear by being honest, brief and adding humor to your introduction."

Miriam Tyson

"I must overcome fear every time I speak. I try to use the introduction as an area to relax. I talk about myself and my job. That seems to help."

David Shaw

"I figure I am the expert on the subject so that puts me one jump ahead of the audience. That bolsters my confidence to give my nerves a boost so that I can step in front of the group to 'Go get 'em.' "

Billie Preston

"The more times you speak the easier it becomes. I would hope that the pre-speech nervousness never leaves. It gives me something to overcome."

Vic Pinckney

"I take a deep breath of air to fill my lungs and then exhale slowly as I am being introduced. A key point I remember as I'm mentally preparing myself is that I know more about the subject I'm speaking on than the people in the audience."

Nancy Garrett

"I was successfully able to overcome my fear of speaking before large groups by constantly reminding myself that only I know the subject material to be presented."

Jerry Critz

"I'm a member of Toastmasters and have found the speeches and workshops have been a great help to me in my public speaking."

Norma Lloyd

"After thinking about my fear of public speaking for a long time, I came to the conclusion that I was well-trained and knew my material and that everyone in my audience respected me for this and wished they could get up in front of people and talk as I did."

Sandra Wilkerson

"I overcame fear by believing in myself and knowing that I was an important person and had something worth saying and worth people hearing."

Ina Mae Elsberry

"Speaking is its own reward. Once one learns the joy resulting from informing and controlling an audience, speaking becomes a pleasure. It is not work, but rather a pastime to be enjoyed."

Tom Beightol

"The thing that can best put you at ease with the group you are speaking to is to BELIEVE IN YOUR MATERIAL — or your message. I have had great response from the groups I've talked to — many have written special 'Thank Yous.' I always remind myself that I am with them because I'm invited and they WANT to hear what I have to say."

Lorma Kunath